Bright Ideas
Easter Activities

Written by Jim Fitzsimmons

Introduction

Traditionally Easter is for many a time for decorating and eating eggs and remembering the resurrection of Christ. Children love to hunt for the eggs hidden by the Easter Bunny which can be made of chocolate or painted and decorated real ones. Cards and gifts are also exchanged. These will give infinitely more pleasure if they are hand-made. *Easter Activities* will show you how. We have included helpful chapters on decorating eggs; recipes; making cards, gifts and decorations. All the ideas can be used as they are, or elaborated or simplified as you wish. There is a useful photocopiable section giving a variety of useful templates and designs.

Many festivals, carnivals and parades are held with the wearing of lavishly decorated hats and bonnets. A number of games and customs are also associated with this time of year so we have incorporated chapters on both these topics.

Easter coincides with spring and other religious festivals of new life and new beginnings. Projects on all aspects of nature, ranging from the simple study of leaves and flowers to making your very own weather-vane, have been included in the chapter on 'Nature at Easter'.

The children's growing excitement as Easter approaches will be enriched by a knowledge of customs and festivals taking place around the world. You will find 'Easter around the world' an invaluable aid to help you do this.

There is a great deal of fun to be gained from Easter and spring preparations. We hope that this book will provide you with the inspiration and information to make it a success.

Jim Fitzsimmons

Contents

Published by Scholastic Publications Ltd, Marlborough House, Holly Walk, Leamington Spa, Warwickshire CV32 4LS

© 1988 Scholastic Publications Ltd.

Written by Jim Fitzsimmons
Edited by Jackie Cunningham-Craig
Sub-edited by Melissa Bellamy
Illustrations by Chris Saunderson

Printed in Great Britain by
Loxley Brothers Ltd, Sheffield

ISBN 0 590 70873 2

Front and back cover: designed by Sue Limb, photographed by Martin Chillmaid

Easter around the world

The word 'Easter' comes from 'Eastre' or 'Eostre', the Anglo Saxon goddess of the dawn whose spring festival was celebrated in April. Before the arrival of Christianity, people believed that the sun died in winter and was born again in spring; on the day of the spring equinox they would sing and dance as the sun rose in the sky.

Many countries took their name for Easter from the Jewish festival of Passover; for example, in France Easter is called Pâques, in Italy Pasqua, in Sweden Pask, in Spain Pascua, in Holland Paach or Pasen, in Denmark Paaske and in Wales Pasg.

The Passover Festival developed partly from the Feast of Unleavened Bread when Jews would destroy the sour dough which was used like yeast to leaven bread, so that the produce of the year to come would be protected. The first sheaf of the newly cut barley was then presented to the priests as a thanksgiving. This feast became combined with another, called Pesach, when Jews would sacrifice a sheep or goat in the spring to give thanks. As a protection against bad luck, the shepherds' tent posts were painted with the blood of the creature.

The name 'Passover' comes from the time when the Jews escaped the punishment received by the Egyptians for enslaving the Jews by painting sheep's blood on their door posts during the Pesach festival. Nowadays, during the Passover Festival, Jews remember the day they escaped from slavery, whilst celebrating release from the grips of winter. They worship in the temple and celebrate at home. The day before Passover, homes are cleaned, leavened bread is thrown away and unleavened bread is baked in preparation for the feast.

The first Easter took place during the Passover feast, which is always celebrated at full moon, so to keep Easter Day on a Sunday it was decided that Easter should always be celebrated on the Sunday following the first full moon after the spring equinox (21 March).

Finding the date of Easter Day

First find the key number by adding one year to the year you are in, then divide by 19; if there is a remainder, this is the key number. For example:

$$\frac{1989 + 1}{19} = 104 \text{ remainder } 14$$

So 14 is the key number.

Now you need to find the Sunday letter. Divide the year you are in by 4, ignoring any remainders or fractions:

$$\frac{1989}{4} = 497$$

Add this number to the year number and then add 6:

$$
\begin{array}{r}
1989 \\
497 \\
+\quad 6 \\
\hline
2492
\end{array}
$$

Divide this number by 7:

$$\frac{2492}{7} = 356$$

If there is no remainder, the Sunday letter is A. For other remainders the letters are as follows: 1 – G, 2 – F, 3 – E, 4 – D, 5 – C, 6 – B. Because we had no remainder, the Sunday letter is A.

Key number		A	B	C	D	E	F	G
						Sunday letters		
1	April	16	17	18	19	20	21	15
2	April	9	10	4	5	6	7	8
3	March	26	27	28	29	30	24	25
4	April	16	17	18	12	13	14	15
5	April	2	3	4	5	6	7	1
6	April	23	24	25	19	20	21	22
7	April	9	10	11	12	13	14	15
8	April	2	3	4	Mar 29	30	31	Apr 1
9	April	23	17	18	19	20	21	22
10	April	9	10	11	12	6	7	8
11	March	26	27	28	29	30	31	Apr 1
12	April	16	17	18	19	20	14	15
13	April	9	3	4	5	6	7	8
14	March	26	27	28	29	23	24	25
15	April	16	17	11	12	13	14	15
16	April	2	3	4	5	6	Mar 31	Apr 1
17	April	23	24	18	19	20	21	22
18	April	9	10	11	12	13	14	8
19	April	2	3	Mar 28	29	30	31	Apr 1

Taken from the *Hippo Easter Book* (Scholastic Publications)

Now look at the chart. The key numbers are down the side, so go down to 14 and then read across to the A column. This will give you the date of Easter for 1989 (26 March).

You can do this for any year up to the year 2100.

Spring festivals

Easter always falls in the spring in the northern hemisphere, and so it came to be associated with new life, and many spring celebrations took place around Easter time. So when people began to leave Europe for Australia, America and Canada, they took with them many of the customs. In Australia and South America where Easter falls at a different season of the year, many of the spring celebrations remained associated with Easter.

Many countries and cultures hold spring festivals around Easter time. The Hindu festival of Holi is a celebration of the arrival of spring, and is associated with happy singing. It falls at the time of the full moon towards the end of February, or in March, around spring harvest time. Large bonfires are lit and images of a legendary character called Holika are made and burned on the fires. Holi lasts for three to five days, during which there are processions, singing and dancing in the streets. Bright clothes are worn and the people spray one another with coloured water or powder in remembrance of the games played by Lord Krishna and the cowherds and milkmaids.

Sikhs celebrate a similar festival called Hola or Hola-Mohalla, said to have begun when Guru Gobind Singh became concerned long ago that the festival of Holi was too rowdy. He gathered all the Sikhs together and they held mock battles and competitions of horsemanship. Hola still involves feats of strength and courage, but now incorporates fun as well, lasting about three days.

Long ago the Chinese held the Lantern Festival (Teng Chieh) on the first full moon of the year to celebrate the new birth of the world. Brightly coloured lanterns (see page 70) were hung everywhere to represent increasing light and warmth after the winter of cold and darkness, lanterns were carried in processions and fireworks were set off. (See page 14 for a Chinese springtime story.) Nowadays some Chinese still celebrate the spring festival of Ch'ing Ming, the Festival of Pure Brightness, about a month after the Lantern Festival took place.

In Japan there is a festival called Setsubun, or Change of Season, celebrated in the temples, the streets and people's homes. Roast beans are scattered in the home and sometimes in the streets to scare away evil spirits.

Around the end of February the birthday of Muhammed is celebrated by Muslims, and Buddha's birthday is also celebrated in the spring.

In Russia, Easter is not officially celebrated, but many Christians observe it privately. The only remnant of Easter is Maslennitsa, an ancient Slavic pagan festival which lasted many days and marked the end of winter and the beginning of farm work for spring. Nowadays the State allows this festival to mark the ending of winter. Since there is still plenty of snow about, the people celebrate with sleigh rides and snowball fights; huge snow sculptures and ice carvings are made, and carnivals, processions, fairs and dances are held. People dress up and go from house to house collecting money, and when night falls, straw figures representing winter are burned on bonfires.

Easter events

Shrove Tuesday, the day before Lent begins, is celebrated in many countries with carnivals, especially in southern Europe, where there are feasts, parties and masquerades. In France the day is known as Mardi Gras or Fat Tuesday, because they would eat up all the fat and butter. In Germany and Switzerland it is known as Fastnacht or Fast Night, when cakes and nuts are eaten.

In Denmark and Norway children traditionally decorate branches of birch with brightly coloured paper streamers, and in Sweden birch twigs and chicken feathers are used to decorate homes.

The word 'Lent' comes from 'lengten', the old English word for 'spring', a time when the days begin to lengthen. In Christian countries, on Ash Wednesday, the first day of Lent, the ashes of the previous year's burned palms, used to celebrate Palm Sunday, are used to make a cross on the foreheads of the people.

Lent lasts for 40 days and 40 nights (from Ash Wednesday to Easter Sunday, not including the Sundays in between), as a reminder of Christ's fasting in the wilderness. During Lent Christians give up something they like to remind them not to be selfish, and perhaps to give the money which has been saved to help others.

At one time calendars were made, rather like Advent calendars, to mark the passing of Lent. In France, paper nun Lenten calendars are still made. The nun has seven feet, one for each week in Lent. The calendar is hung by a thread and at the end of each week, one of her feet is tucked under.

The Greek Lenten calendar is called a kukaras, and is made from a large well-scrubbed potato and feathers. A hole is made right through the centre of the potato using a skewer or knitting needle. A piece of string is then threaded through the hole and knotted at the end, so that the potato can be hung. Seven large feathers are stuck into the potato, and one is pulled out at the end of each

week in Lent. Instead of real ones, feathers could be made out of paper and cocktail sticks.

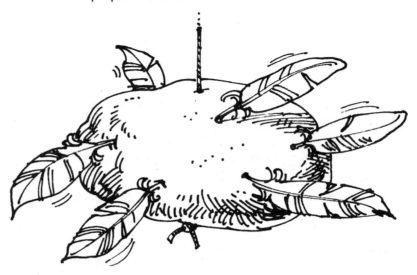

Passion plays are performed at Oberammergau in Germany and at Pernambuco in Brazil, about the trial and death of Jesus, which is remembered on Passion Sunday (the fifth Sunday in Lent).

Palm Sunday is so-called because Jesus is said to have ridden into Jerusalem on a donkey just before His death, welcomed by the people waving palm branches. Churches are decorated with palm branches on this day; in Britain people used to go 'a palming' two or three days before Palm Sunday, to collect yew, hazel or willow branches, since palm trees do not grow in northern countries.

In Spain some cities have processions every evening during the week before Easter, a custom which was also introduced to Mexico and South America when they were conquered by Spain.

On Maundy Thursday, the day when Jesus was said to have washed the feet of his disciples, a tradition developed in Britain, Austria, Russia, France and Spain for rich or noble people to give money or food to the poor. In Britain, Queen Victoria began the custom of giving specially minted money in white leather bags, with more money in small red bags instead of food. The present queen continues this tradition, giving maundy coins in a white purse (one coin for each year of her reign) and some extra money in a red purse. The money is given to old people – one man and one woman for each year of the Queen's age.

In the Middle East, Armenian and Syrian Christians still hold foot-washing ceremonies where priests wash the feet of beggars and offer them gifts.

The word 'maundy' comes from the Latin word 'mandatum' which means 'command', since this was the day on which Jesus gave his disciples a new commandment – to 'love one another'.

Good Friday is the day on which Jesus died. In Eastern churches it is known as Great Friday, and in Germany Silent Friday since no bells ring. The next day is a day of preparation for Easter in many parts of the world. In Poland, Hungary and Czechoslovakia, the first egg to be decorated usually shows a ploughshare to remind people of the beginning of farmwork in spring. In Lithuania, large hollow artificial eggs are made with a hole in each end. Inside, modelled in fondant, are spring scenes of tiny hills, trees, bushes, rabbits and chickens.

In parts of Germany and Yugoslavia, children make nests of moss in the garden, hoping that the Easter Hare will find them and fill them with eggs the next day. At one time, in the Hartz mountains of Germany, giant wooden wheels covered in straw were set alight and rolled down the slopes. The fields in which they came to rest would supposedly produce good crops.

In Sicily Easter is celebrated on the Saturday, because the Sicilians say that their part of Italy is nearer to Palestine, so the news of the resurrection reached them first.

Activity

Split the class into groups and give each one an area for display – these could be grouped around a map of the world. Encourage the children to find out about Easter in other countries – the foods, customs and traditions, games and pastimes, and to display their findings in the form of illustrations, writing or objects made or brought from home. They could make some of the traditional items connected with their chosen country, such as Easter trees, Easter baskets or decorated eggs.

In the United States some people stay awake all night waiting for the sun to rise. In some parts of Africa, young women dressed in white go from house to house at dawn singing Easter hymns to wake people on Easter morning.

To celebrate the arrival of spring, Easter parades often take place on Easter Sunday afternoon, where people can wear new clothes as a sign of the changing seasons, and competitions are held to find the best Easter bonnet. Traditionally, large Easter parades are held in Battersea Park, London, and Atlantic City, New Jersey.

Easter Monday is a national holiday in many countries, when games and sports are played. In Sydney, Australia, the Royal Easter Show is held – an enormous agricultural show with displays of flowers, fruit and vegetables, cattle, sheep, and art and craft. This is followed by a huge fun-fair and firework display in the evening.

Lo-Hi and the Dragon of Winter

Long ago in China there lived a fisherman named Lo-Hi. He lived alone in a small hut on the edge of the lake where he fished. He worked hard and each morning he would take his fish to the nearby village to sell. Lo-Hi made enough money to live comfortably and save a little regularly. In the market he had seen a fine jacket of black satin on the back of which, embroidered in brightly coloured silks, was a design which looked like a monstrous face. Lo-Hi had wanted this jacket from the moment he first saw it and while he was saving he was worried that someone else would buy it. However, he had soon saved enough and the jacket was his. How proud he

felt as he walked home and how all his friends and neighbours admired it.

Life was good in the village by the lake and Lo-Hi was happy. In those days the weather was always fine. It was never too hot, never too cold, never too wet and never too dry, but one day all this changed. The weather became colder and colder, and the crops began to wither

and die. Even the lake began to freeze over so Lo-Hi could not fish. Huge grey clouds filled the sky and hid the sun.

Soon nothing would grow at all. One day there was a great noise in the sky. People rushed indoors, but Lo-Hi stayed to see what would happen. He was amazed to see a huge silver dragon flying through the air. As it soared high and low, showers of hail and snow scattered over the ground below. Soon the earth was cold and frozen and covered with a carpet of white.

Lo-Hi watched as the dragon flew to the top of a nearby mountain.

One by one the villagers came out of their houses. They had never seen snow before and they listened as Lo-Hi explained what had happened.

At first the villagers enjoyed the snow and they had great fun, but each day the dragon would fly down the mountain bringing the bad weather to the village and soon food was getting scarce and people began to get worried. A meeting was called and it was decided that

Lo-Hi was to go up the mountain and try to persuade the dragon to leave.

Lo-Hi agreed to go, and he wore his strongest shoes, and because he wanted to look important he wore his beautiful new jacket.

It was a long, hard journey over ground covered with snow and frozen with ice. At last he reached the top of the mountain.

'Hello!' he shouted. All was quiet except for his own echo. He tried again and almost immediately he was answered by a booming voice. 'Who dares call on the Dragon of Winter?' 'It is I, Lo-Hi, I have come to ask you to leave. Since you came here nothing will grow, the clouds you make stop the sun shining, the lake is frozen and I cannot fish – we are all starving.' 'Ha! that is nothing to me', laughed the dragon. 'I like it here and I mean to stay. There is nothing you can do about it so leave here at once, or else!!' So saying the dragon roared loudly and blew fiercely at Lo-Hi.

He blew so hard that Lo-Hi's jacket was torn from his back and it flew up into the air shaking and flapping. As it was buffeted by the dragon's breath it turned round and round until at last the fierce face was just in front of the dragon's nose. He had never seen anything like it before and with a muffled roar the dragon rose into the air and disappeared over the top of the mountain.

Lo-Hi seized his chance and ran for his life. He ran all the way down the mountain and did not stop until he reached his hut.

His encounter with the dragon, although it had scared him, had also given him an idea. Wasting no time, he got two strips of bamboo and tied them together in the form of a cross. Then he stretched a piece of silk over the frame. He sewed the edges and added a tail and a long string. Then he painted the most horrible face that he could imagine on the front. He had made a kite.

Next day he showed the villagers and persuaded them to make lots of kites. Lo-Hi explained his plan.

The next time the dragon flew down blowing and scattering snow, Lo-Hi and the villagers sent up their kites. The kites looked like a great army of angry monsters and at first the dragon was scared as before, but then he returned and started to do battle with them. He blew and blew, but the more he blew the more the kites bobbed angrily. The dragon blew and blew again, but he still could not overcome the kites. At last, exhausted, he fell out of the sky and with a tremendous crash, shook the ground as he landed.

He lay still on the snow covered ground. The grey clouds disappeared and the sun came out shining strong and clear.

'Hooray!!' shouted the villagers, 'the Dragon of Winter is dead!' Lo-Hi saw a movement and quickly realised that the dragon was not dead, but merely exhausted and stunned.

'I will never give up', gasped the dragon as he struggled to his feet. 'I will fight and fight.'

'But if you stay here you will have to fight every day, and we will not give up either', said Lo-Hi.

'Then what is to be done?' asked the dragon. 'I too need somewhere to live. Am I to blame for bringing snow and ice? This is what I am made of. Without it I will die!'

'We will die if you stay here', shouted the villagers. 'Wait', shouted Lo-Hi, 'we must make an agreement.' He turned to the dragon and said, 'What if you stay for half

of the year, and then find somewhere else for the rest of the time. That will give us a chance to grow food, and this we can store, to be eaten during the time you are here.'

The dragon thought for a while and then reluctantly agreed. 'I will return', he called, as he flew off over the horizon.

The weather became warmer and once more new life returned to the fields and forests and Lo-Hi returned to his fishing. For six months, life was just as before, but after this the weather began to change, more and more

clouds appeared in the sky, and the days grew shorter and colder. The villagers knew that the Dragon of Winter was returning.

Because they had stored their food the villagers were able to get over the cold months but they longed for the day when the Dragon of Winter would leave. If the villagers thought that the dragon had stayed too long they would get out their kites once more and the sight of them would remind the dragon that it was time for him to move on.

Now every year people in many countries fly kites on those windy days of February and March. Who knows? Maybe they are being flown to chase away the Dragon of Winter!

J Fitzsimmons

Simple kite

Age group
Seven plus.

Group size
Small groups.

What you need
Cane (6mm in diameter) or
bamboo canes split down the middle,
linen, plastic or paper, thick thread or string.

What to do
Use two pieces of cane (60 cm and 40 cm long) to construct the frame. About one seventh of the way down the longest cane, position the smaller cane to make a cross piece. Tie the two canes together with thread or string (see diagram). Linen, plastic or paper can be used for the kite covering. Staple or sew pockets at each corner of the kite for the frame ends to fit into.

Add a tail by tying strips of material at intervals on a length of string. If you make a plastic kite, staple a long strip of 2 cm wide plastic to the bottom corner of the kite. Attach a kite string to the cross section of the canes.

REMEMBER: Split cane can be very sharp so be very careful.

Decorating eggs

All children love to decorate eggs at Easter time to make for themselves or as gifts. They provide an enormous amount of pleasure plus the opportunity to use their creativity and imagination.

In Poland, Hungary and Czechoslovakia, a great deal of care is taken over decorating eggs. In Poland the eggs are called 'pysanki' which means to scratch. The eggs are first blown to remove the contents and then covered in beeswax. A design is scratched into the wax, the eggs are soaked in dye, and the beeswax is loosened by gently heating the eggs. When the wax is wiped away the design is revealed and varnishing completes the egg.

The children can work with blown eggs or hard-boiled eggs. These are best prepared in advance by the teacher. To make blown eggs, pierce both ends with a pin making one hole slightly larger than the other. Place a finger and thumb over the holes and shake the egg hard to break the yolk, taking care not to break the shell. Hold the egg over a bowl and blow through the smaller hole until all the contents are removed. Then place the empty eggshell under a fast-flowing tap to rinse it out. Allow the water to drain out and let the eggshell dry thoroughly.

Blown eggs may be too delicate for children to handle, so it is probably best to boil the eggs for about half an hour in salted water (to make sure they don't crack).

Dyed eggs

Age range
Seven plus.

Group size
Individuals.

What you need
Clean hard-boiled or blown eggs, vinegar, salad oil, fabric dyes, or any of the following for preparing dyes: yellow — onion peel, caraway seed, saffron; brown — tea or coffee, onion peel, oak bark; red — onion peel and vinegar, beet juice; green — spinach, nettle roots and leaves; blue — mallow, logwood; black or grey — alder wood, alder pussies.

What to do
To prepare the dye, boil the materials in water until it is fairly dark. The liquid may be strained through cheesecloth or muslin, and by adding a little vinegar the colours will be slightly more luminous.

Leave the eggs in the dye until they are the right shade — a shorter time will give a paler shade and a longer time will give a darker shade. When the eggs have been dyed and allowed to dry, they can be rubbed with a drop of salad oil to protect the colours and add a shine.

Scratching

Age range
Seven plus.

Group size
Individuals.

What you need
Dyed hard-boiled or blown eggs, metal instrument with point (nail-file or nail).

What to do
Simply scratch designs into the surface of the dyed eggs (see page 19) using a sharp-pointed instrument. The eggs could be partitioned in any of the following ways with smaller designs of scrolls or flowers made inside these areas.

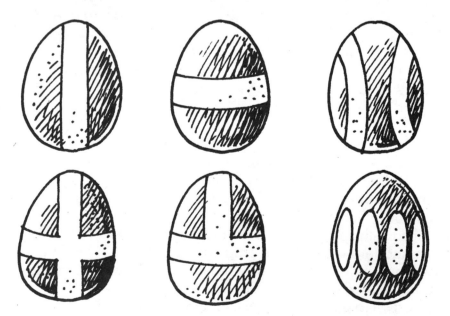

Blocking

Age range
Seven plus.

Group size
Individuals.

What you need
Undyed hard-boiled or blown eggs, small flowers or grasses, ferns or herbs, salad oil, egg white or vegetable glue, feet from pair of tights, dye.

What to do
Dip the flowers, grasses, ferns or herbs in salad oil, egg white or vegetable glue, and arrange them on the surface of the undyed egg. Wrap the egg in the cut-off foot of a pair of tights, knotting the material to keep the egg in place.

Place the egg in the dye and leave it until it is the right shade, then take it out and remove the material and the grasses etc. The eggshell will be white where the plant was positioned and coloured elsewhere.

Try wrapping the egg in an onion skin to produce a marbled effect.

Batik

Age range
Seven plus.

Group size
Individuals.

What you need
Undyed hard-boiled or blown eggs, wax crayons or paintbrush and melted wax from candle, dye.

What to do
Make a design on the egg using wax crayons or a paintbrush dipped in melted wax dripped from either a lighted candle or a wax crayon heated over a candle flame. Dip the egg in the dye for as long as necessary, then remove the wax by holding the egg at the side of a candle flame (if you hold it near the top of the flame, soot will form on the egg). Soak up the wax with a soft cloth as it melts, and do not scratch the surface of the egg or the design may be spoiled.

This process can be repeated up to five times with different colours of dye. Leave the wax on, adding more to the design each time, and work from the lighter to the darker shades: ie white (natural eggshell), yellow, orange, light red, dark red, blue, violet, black.

Note: An adult should always be present when children are working with burning candles or molten wax.

Wax dripping

Age range
Seven plus.

Group size
Individuals.

What you need
Dyed or undyed hard-boiled or blown eggs, wax crayons, candle.

What to do
Melt different-coloured wax crayons in a candle flame and drip them on to the egg. Fluorescent crayons make particularly bright eggs.

Striped eggs

Age range
Seven plus.

Group size
Individuals.

What you need
Hard-boiled or blown eggs,
scraps of yarn,
PVA adhesive.

What to do
Brush the egg with adhesive in the areas where the yarn is to go, then wind the yarn round the egg vertically until you have the desired width, keeping the strands close together.

adhesive and, starting in the middle, wind a spiral of yarn on to it. A matchstick can be used to push the strands into place.

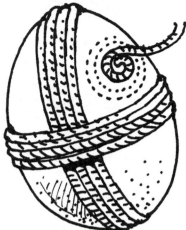

Allow time between each stage for the glue to dry or the yarn might be dislodged as the egg is handled.
Here are some designs to try:

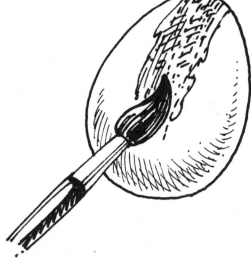

Add a horizontal band of yarn in the same way, then add small spirals of yarn in a contrasting colour – mark the position of each spiral lightly in pencil, coat it with

Yarn eggs

Age range
Seven plus.

Group size
Individuals.

What you need
Brown hard-boiled or blown eggs, metallic yarn or plastic beading thread, clear glue.

What to do
Make a small hole in the base and top of the egg (if you are not using blown eggs). Spread a little glue around the base of the shell and push the ends of the yarn into the base hole. Wind the yarn in a spiral around the shell adding more glue as you work up the shell. Take care to keep the spiral even and level. At the top twist the spiral over the hole and insert the end into the hole.

Strings of beads can be used in the same way, but a stronger glue may be necessary to keep them in place. The application will take longer since each row will need to dry, otherwise the beads will fall off or become covered with glue. However, if it is done carefully, the result will be most rewarding.

Cutting eggs

Age range
Seven to twelve.

Group size
Small groups with adult help.

What you need
For each group: a goose or hen's egg (raw), a wire scouring pad, fine sandpaper, an elastic band, a pencil, a junior hacksaw, a sharp knife, a container for the contents of the egg, newspaper, old cotton reels, a cardboard box (eg a shoe box), car spray paint, scraps of silky fabric, sewing thread, latex adhesive for gluing fabric, epoxy adhesive for gluing on the hinge, masking tape, a hinge, materials for decoration (narrow lace ribbon and braid, small pearls, sequins, old junk jewellery, transfers, beads etc), an egg stand.

What to do
Cutting the egg requires patience and a steady hand – it might be best for an adult to do this part, allowing the children to mark the egg and then decorate it once it is cut.

Clean the egg with a scouring pad and if the goose egg is rough, smooth it with fine sandpaper.

Put an elastic band around the egg, either horizontally or vertically, and draw a line close to it with a pencil. Hold the egg and rub gently round the pencil line with a

hacksaw blade to make a groove. Continue until the membrane of the egg is visible, then cut the membrane with a sharp knife (this should be done by an adult). Empty the contents of the egg into a container, rinse the shell in cold water and allow it to dry. Further cuts should be marked out and made in the same way.

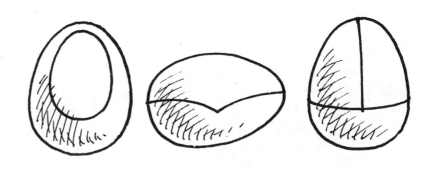

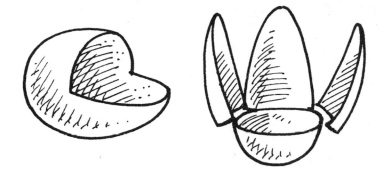

Instead of making a lining, you could paint the inside of the egg.

Use masking tape to hold the egg sections together until the hinge is stuck in place. Scrape the paint away from the area where the hinge is to be fixed, stick on the hinge and leave the glue to dry for 24 hours. Then remove the tape and check that the egg opens freely.

Decorate the outside of the egg with braid, ribbon, beads or sequins, and place a sprig of silk or tissue flowers, small sugared almonds or chocolate eggs inside it.

Cover the table with newspaper and stand the egg sections, rounded side up, on cotton reels inside a box on the table. Spray the sections lightly with paint and allow them to dry for at least an hour. Spray each section two or three times to ensure an even coating of paint. (Make sure there is good ventilation when spraying.)

Cut a piece of fabric to fit inside the egg and work a row of gathering stitches close to the edge of the fabric. Put a line of latex glue round the inside edge of the egg and ease the lining into it, pulling up the gathering thread. Press the lining into place, pull out the thread and glue on a strip of lace to conceal the raw edges of the lining.

Egg stands can be bought from most craft shops or made from a section of the inner cardboard tube of a kitchen roll, a cotton reel or a bottle top, painted or covered with a strip of ribbon.

A curtain ring with a strip of fused pearls glued around it also makes an attractive stand. A lump of Plasticine will add stability to the stand.

Eggshell paperweights

Age range
Six to twelve.

Group size
Individuals.

What you need
Eggshell with the end
broken off,
a card ring cut
from cardboard tube,
modelling plaster,
poster paint,
matchsticks.

What to do
Support the shell on a card ring and fill it with modelling
plaster mixed with water to a creamy consistency. When
the plaster is hard, rub the end of the egg on a flat stone
until you get a perfectly flat surface and the egg stands
upright unsupported. There is no need to remove the
eggshell unless the edges are still uneven.

Using bright colours, decorate the paperweight with a
pattern to cover the whole shell. For example, paint small
triangles or make a simple floral pattern made by
dabbing on groups of dots with the end of a matchstick
dipped in paint.

Painted eggs

Age range
Six plus.

Group size
Individuals.

What you need
Hard-boiled or blown eggs, poster paints or felt-tipped
pens, sequins, thread or ribbon, a matchstick or bead.

What to do
Blown or hard-boiled eggs can be painted or decorated
using poster paints, felt-tipped pens etc. The egg surface
may be partitioned in any of the ways mentioned in
'Scratching' (page 20), and the different sections
coloured with poster paints or felt-tipped pens.

Using a gold or silver felt-tipped pen the main areas of
pattern can be outlined, and a few sequins can be stuck
on to the surface for an extra sparkle.

The eggs can be hung as mobiles or from an Easter tree in any of the following ways:

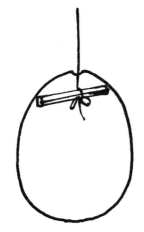

with a matchstick

with a length of ribbon

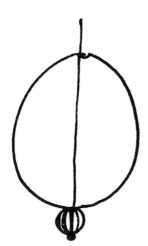

with a bead

Hedgehog

Age range
Six to twelve.

Group size
Small groups or individuals.

What you need
Hard-boiled or blown eggs, card, latex adhesive, brown paint, pieces of bark, thorns from the stem of a rose bush, beads.

What to do
Apply latex adhesive to the blunt end of the thorns and stick these over the upper surface of the eggshell. The small beads may be used as eyes and a nose, and when the adhesive is dry, paint on the whiskers and the tips of the thorns with brown paint. Make four small clawed feet out of card and stick these to the bottom of the hedgehog, then glue the model on to the piece of bark.

A Red Indian

Age range
Six to twelve.

Group size
Small groups or individuals.

What you need
Blown eggs, a junior hacksaw, felt-tipped pens, latex adhesive, stiff paper, beads, small feathers, scraps of lace, egg boxes, wool.

What to do
Take one of the eggshells and carefully cut it in two using the junior hacksaw. Use the larger of the two pieces as the base of the Indian's head-dress, and decorate it using felt-tipped pens. Stick the head-dress on to the top of the second piece of eggshell, like a hat, make a plait from the wool and glue this at the back.

Draw on a face, make ears from paper and stick these in place. Use beads for the eyes and nose, and glue the feathers on to the head-dress. Hide the ends of the feathers and the joint between the two eggshell halves by sticking a scrap of lace around the head as a headband. The Red Indian may be displayed by gluing him to the inverted section of an egg box.

There are many variations on this theme and a whole family of eggheads can be made.

An Easter rabbit

Age range
Six to twelve.

Group size
Small groups
or individuals.

What you need
Hard-boiled or blown eggs,
card, PVA adhesive,
cotton wool, paint.

What to do
Make a card ring and glue this to one end of the egg,
then cut a V-shaped piece of card for the feet (see
figure 1), two strips of card for the arms (see figure 2),
and two ears with slits in the bottom of each so that they
can be glued to the curved surface of the egg (see
figure 3).

Figure 1

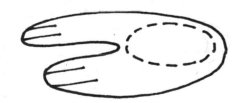

Figure 2

Figure 3

Assemble the rabbit as shown in figure 4, paint it and
cut out eyes, nose and teeth from paper. Stick these in
place, paint on whiskers and stick on a cotton-wool tail.

Figure 4

29

An Easter chick

Age range
Six to twelve.

Group size
Small groups
or individuals.

What you need
Hard-boiled or
blown eggs,
card,
PVA adhesive,
yellow and
orange paint.

What to do
Make a card ring and glue this to the egg so that it points
at an angle (see figure 1), and cut out V-shaped feet from
the card.

Figure 1

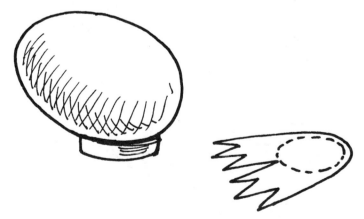

Make a fan-shaped tail, two triangular wings and a
beak from the card, and stick them in place. Colour the
model with yellow paint, then paint the feet and inside of
the beak orange.

With a little imagination the eggs can be transformed
into all kinds of animal, as models or mobiles.

Egg balloons

Age range
Seven to eleven.

Group size
Small groups.

What you need
Eggshells,
poster paints,
plastic mesh
vegetable bags,
corks,
strips of paper.

What to do
Paint each eggshell in bright colours, using stripes,
diamonds, rings or squares. Glue the egg by its top inside
a mesh vegetable bag (see figure 1).

Figure 1

Put a piece of cork inside the neck of the bag and tie it
in place with sewing thread (see figure 2).

Figure 2

Glue a strip of paper round the cork, then snip off the
surplus net (see figure 3). As a finishing touch, mount a
paper flag on a pin and push it into the cork (see
figure 4).

Figure 3

Figure 4

The finished balloons can be hung separately or
grouped to hang together from wire coat-hangers as
mobiles.

Candle moulds

Age range
Seven to eleven.

Group size
Small group with adult supervision.

What you need
Blown eggs,
matchsticks,
Plasticine,
milk bottles,
wax,
wicks.

What to do
Cut the end off a blown egg and thread the wick through the hole in the other end. Secure the wick, block the hole with Plasticine and hold the wick in place at the top of the egg by tying it to a matchstick (see figure 1).

Figure 1

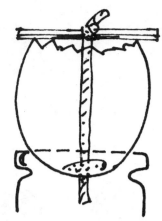

Pour in the molten wax with great care— an adult should do this or supervise closely. Different-coloured layers of wax can be poured into the shell, tilting the egg as each layer goes in to achieve different effects and designs. Plain candles can be decorated by adding pieces of fern or pressed flowers which are dipped in hot wax and then stuck on to the side of the candle. The candle's surface may be textured by using the end of a nail, screw or rivet which has been heated in a candle flame and then pressed into the surface of the candle to build up a pattern.

To remove the candle from the mould, crack the shell like a hard-boiled egg. Trim the wick and base and group the candles together to make a display.

Egg and cress characters

Age range
Five to twelve.

Group size
Small groups.

What you need
Large eggshells with the
ends broken off,
paints,
felt-tipped pens,
varnish, pipe-cleaners,
scraps of material,
bin liner scraps,
mustard or cress seeds,
cotton wool.

What to do
Younger children can concentrate on decorating the
eggshell, but older ones may like to try making a body to
go with their egghead.

Carefully wash the empty shell to remove all traces of
egg yolk and leave it to dry. Then encourage children to
use their imaginations to create a character, such as a
space monster or clown.

Colour the features with bright felt-tipped pens or
acrylic paints and apply a coat of varnish to give added
depth and shine to the colours and to strengthen the shell.

When the character is finished, soak a small piece of
cotton wool in water and carefully place it inside the
shell. Sprinkle mustard or cress seeds evenly over the
surface of the cotton wool, and water frequently.

After about ten days, the eggheads will have a full
head of 'hair'.

Eggshell flowers

Age range
Five to twelve.

Group size
Small groups
or individuals.

What you need
Broken eggshells, thin wire, pipe-cleaners or cocktail
sticks, strong adhesive, thick powder colours or poster
paints, clay or Plasticine.

What to do
Attach small broken pieces of eggshell to stems of thin
wire, pipe-cleaners or cocktail sticks using a blob of
strong adhesive.

Paint the shell flowers and push them into a bed of clay
or Plasticine inside an eggshell bowl.

Eggshell caterpillar

Age range
Five to twelve.

Group size
Small groups or individuals.

What you need
Eggshells,
strong adhesive
or string,
thick powder colours
or poster paints.

What to do
Use eggshells with the ends broken off, paint them and join them together using glue or string threaded through. Paint on features at one end to complete the caterpillar.

34

Exotic eggs

Age range
Five to twelve.

Group size
Small groups
or individuals.

What you need
Empty plastic squeezy
lemons, adhesive,
enamel nail varnish
or gold or silver
aerosol paint,
split peas
or pasta shapes,
sequins.

What to do
An empty plastic lemon can be decorated to look just like a very exotic egg, but it is much easier to handle. First you have to get rid of the bump made by the lid, so unscrew the cap and pull out the inner covering (the piece with the hole through which the lemon is squeezed). Cut off the whole piece just below the cap and push the inner covering back into the hole – it should fit exactly.

Cover the lemon a little at a time with glue and stick on split peas as close together as possible until the whole of the lemon is covered. When the glue has dried, the whole thing can be painted with enamel nail varnish or gold or silver aerosol paint.

You could use small macaroni, pasta circles or, if the lemon is painted first, small dried flowers or sequins.

Decorative egg holder

Age range
Six plus.

Group size
Individuals.

What you need
Card,
scissors,
paints or
felt-tipped pens.

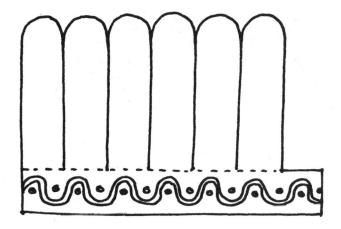

What to do
Cut a card base as shown. Form it into a circle and roll the petals around a pencil to give them a curved shape. Paint or decorate the egg and place it into the base.

Easter recipes

From Pancake Day to Easter Monday, the Easter period has numerous traditional recipes for children to try.

As Lent was introduced as a time of fasting, pancakes, coquille buns (in Norwich) or baldock doughnuts (in Hertfordshire), were made on Shrove Tuesday to use up the flour and eggs. Pancakes are still made in many countries, while in Italy, pretzels are eaten instead.

On the fourth Sunday in Lent (Mothering Sunday), simnel cakes are baked and, at one time, a sweet porridge called frumenty was made. On Palm Sunday, fig pies were a traditional midday meal, and hot cross buns are still eaten in most homes on Good Friday.

Children also enjoy baking Easter biscuits cut to any shape they like, such as rabbits, chickens, eggs, and so on.

In Italy, Easter dove cakes are made. These are shaped like a dove after the legend about a king who wanted to capture a city but his horse refused to gallop into battle until a girl offered him a cake shaped like a dove. This reminded the king of the dove of peace, and so he changed his mind and decided not to conquer the city.

The last three recipes are from Norway and from the Jewish Passover festival. Norwegian chicken buns are baked at Easter, while Jews celebrate the Passover with a ceremonial meal called the Seder, which includes a dish called Charoseth and coconut pyramids.

Pancakes

Age range
Nine plus.

Group size
Small groups or
individuals with adult help.

What you need
(for 12 pancakes)
100g plain flour,
2 eggs,
300ml milk,
a pinch of salt,
1 tbsp oil,
1 tbsp white vegetable fat.

What to do
Sieve the salt and flour into a basin and make a small
well in the middle. Crack the eggs into the hollow. Slowly
add half the milk and mix with a wooden spoon to get rid
of the lumps.

Keep mixing until it is quite smooth, and then add the
rest of the milk. Just before the pancakes are to be
cooked stir in the oil. Melt just enough fat to grease the
pan until it is very hot, then put in about two tablespoons
of the mixture all over the bottom of the pan.

Cook at a medium heat until the underside is brown.
Check this by gently lifting the mixture, then turn over.

If you toss it make sure you can catch it in the pan.

Keep the cooked pancakes warm, by putting them
between two plates over a pan of simmering water.

Serve them with lemon juice, sugar, honey or maple
syrup. Alternatively you can make savoury fillings and
roll the pancakes around them.

Coquille buns

Age range
Nine plus.

Group size
Small groups
or individuals
with adult help.

What you need
450g self-raising flour,
50g lard,
50g margarine,
100g sugar,
2 tsps mixed spice,
2 tbsps mixed dried fruit,
1 egg,
a small amount of milk.

What to do
Rub the lard, margarine and the flour together using your
fingers.

Mix in the sugar, spice and fruit. Beat the egg and add
this with a little milk to the mixture to make a soft dough.

Roll out the mixture to a thickness of 5 cm on a floured
board and cut it into squares. If you wish to be really
authentic, cut them in the shape of a scallop shell.

Bake them in a moderate oven (375°F/190°C/gas
mark 5) for about 20 minutes or until golden brown.

Serve them split and buttered.

Baldock doughnuts

Age range
Nine upwards.

Group size
Small groups or individuals with adult help.

What you need
1 large cup of granulated sugar,
1 large cup of milk,
50g butter,
2 small eggs,
1 handful of currants,
1½ tsps cream of tartar,
a small amount of flour,
¼ tsp bicarbonate of soda.

What to do
Mix all the dry ingredients together and then add the milk and beaten eggs. Add just enough flour to make a manageable paste.

Roll the mixture into small balls remembering that they will double their size when cooked.

Fry in deep fat until they are a dark golden brown. Then roll the doughnuts in sugar and serve immediately.

Pretzels

Age range
Nine plus.

Group size
Small groups or individuals with adult help.

What you need
1 packet of dried yeast,
1 cup of lukewarm water,
3 cups of plain flour,
2 tsps baking powder,
a pinch of salt,
1 egg.

What to do
Put the yeast into the water and stir until it dissolves. Leave for 15 minutes.

Put the flour, baking powder and salt into a bowl and then slowly add the yeast and water. Beat the egg in another bowl and then add this to the mixture. Work all the mixture into a dough. If it is too soft add a little more flour.

Knead the dough well on a board which has been covered with flour, then put it in a bowl, cover it with a damp cloth and leave it for about 30 minutes. By this time it will have risen. Knead it again on the floured board.

Roll it out fairly thinly then cut it into strips about 15 cm long and 2 cm wide. Twist the strips of dough into knots.

Leave these on a board and then boil a pan of water. Place three pretzels in the pan when the water is boiling. They will sink, but when they float to the surface again, lift them out and place them on a greased baking tray. Repeat with all the pretzels. Then brush them with beaten egg and bake in a hot oven (450°F/230°C/gas mark 7) for about 15 minutes.

Eat them hot or cold with butter.

Simnel cake

Age range
Nine plus.

Group size
Small groups or individuals with adult help.

What you need
125g margarine,
1 large can of condensed milk,
700g mixed dried fruit,
100g halved glacé cherries,
2 eggs,
200g self-raising flour,
3 tsps mixed spice,
a pinch of salt,
700g marzipan,
apricot jam.

What to do
Preheat the oven to 350°F/180°C/gas mark 4.

Pour a large can of condensed milk into a large saucepan.

Add the margarine, the mixed dried fruit and the glacé cherries.

Heat gently until the margarine melts then simmer gently for 5 minutes. Let it cool then beat in the eggs.

Mix in a bowl the flour, mixed spice and a pinch of salt.

Beat in the fruit mixture. When it is well mixed spread it into a lined 20 cm diameter deep cake tin. Put it into the oven and bake for 45 minutes. Reduce the heat to 300°F/150°C/gas mark 2, and bake for a further hour. Leave it for 10 minutes and then turn it out of the tin.

Roll out 600g marzipan into two 20 cm circles. Slice the cake horizontally and place a circle of marzipan through the centre. Brush the top of the cake with apricot jam then lay the remaining marzipan on top.

Score the top and flute the edge. Then roll 100g marzipan into 11 balls. Secure these to the cake with beaten egg. Glaze the top of the marzipan with egg and brown under a hot grill.

Frumenty

Age range
Seven plus.

Group size
Small groups or individuals with adult help.

What you need
50g clean wheat
soaked overnight in water,
250ml milk,
flavourings such as spices,
chocolate or raspberry etc,
2 tbsps sugar.

What to do
Separate the wheat from the water and put the wheat into a pan with the milk.

Bring to the boil, then let it simmer while stirring with a wooden spoon, until the milk has thickened.

Add the other ingredients and cook for another two minutes, adding more milk if needed. It can be eaten hot or cold.

Years ago frumenty was made by boiling fat wheat grains in water until a jelly formed. The mixture was then put into a large pot with milk, sugar, eggs and sultanas and lightly cooked. This was then poured into dishes and warmed in the oven and served on Mothering Sunday.

Fig pie

Age range
Nine plus.

Group size
Small groups with adult help.

What you need
A pastry shell
(previously cooked),
2 cups of cooked figs,
(if dried figs are used they
should be soaked in water
overnight and then cooked),
¼ cup of currants,
¾ cup of sugar,
½ tsp mixed spice,
1 tbsp orange rind,
1 tbsp treacle or syrup,
2 egg whites.

What to do
Cut the figs into small pieces and add the currants, sugar,
treacle, spices and orange rind.
   Beat the egg whites until stiff. Fold these into the
mixture and mix well.
   Pour the mixture into the baked pastry shell and bake
in a medium oven (375°F/190°C/gas mark 5) for about 20
minutes or until golden brown.

Hot cross buns

Age range
Nine plus.

Group size
Small groups or individuals with adult help.

What you need
(for 12 buns)

For the buns:
100g margarine,
100g caster sugar,
200g self-raising flour,
150g sultanas,
½ tsp mixed spice,
a pinch of salt,
a little milk.

For the crosses:
25g margarine,
50g self-raising flour,
1 dsp water.

Easter biscuits

Age range
Seven plus.

Group size
Small groups or individuals with adult help.

What you need
250g flour,
100g butter,
100g sugar,
50g currants,
½ tsp mixed spice,
lemon juice,
1 egg.

What to do
Since these buns are made without yeast they are not true buns, but they can be made quickly and the mark of the cross makes them special for Good Friday.

Mix all the dry ingredients for the buns into a bowl with the milk until it is a smooth mixture. Form it into small balls and place these on a greased baking tray. They should be slightly flattened and spaced fairly wide apart.

Mix all the ingredients for the crosses and knead for about 2 minutes.

Roll out the mixture on to a floured board and cut into very thin strips about 5 cm long. Two strips can be placed in the form of a cross on the top of each uncooked bun.

Bake for 12 minutes in a hot oven (450°F/230°C/gas mark 7).

They may be eaten hot or cold, cut in two horizontally and spread with butter.

What to do
Rub the butter and flour together. Add the sugar, currants, mixed spice and a few drops of lemon juice, and mix together.

Beat the egg in a cup or small jug and stir this into the mixture.

Turn out the dough on to a floured board and roll it out thinly. Cut out shapes with a pastry cutter or make a rabbit template (see page 104). Use raisins for the eyes and nose.

Place the shapes on a greased baking tray and prick them with a fork. Bake them for about 20 minutes at 350°F/180°C/gas mark 4.

Remove them from the oven and sprinkle them with sugar, then leave to cool.

Italian dove cake

Age range
Nine plus.

Group size
Small groups or individuals with adult help.

What you need
2 pieces of sponge cake large enough to cut into two
dove shapes,
1 carton of sweetened whipping cream,
fruit flavoured syrup
(the kind you put on ice-cream),
white of an egg,
water,
250g icing sugar,
card.

What to do
Make a dove template using photocopiable page 105.
Use the template to cut two dove shapes from the pieces
of sponge cake. Then whip the cream until it is stiff and
spread this over one dove shape. Put the other shape
on top.

Put the egg white into a bowl and beat it with a fork.
Add the icing sugar, a spoonful at a time. Add about
three spoonfuls of water before it gets stiff and the syrup
to make the mixture change colour.

Add more icing sugar until the mixture is nearly stiff
then spread it over the top of the dove cake.

Norwegian chicken buns

Age range
Nine plus.

Group size
Small groups or individuals with adult help.

What you need
(for 12 chicks)
450g strong bread flour,
1 tsp salt,
300ml lukewarm milk,
small knob of butter,
melted easybake yeast (follow
instructions on packet).

What to do
Work all the ingredients into a dough and knead
vigorously for about 10 minutes.

Divide the dough into 12 pieces and roll them into fat
sausage shapes about 10cm long. Make a knot of each
sausage shape.

Push in two currants for eyes and a piece of glacé
cherry for a beak. Place them on a greased baking sheet
and cover with a cloth. Leave them in a warm place for
about an hour or until they double in size.

Brush each chick with beaten egg and bake in a very
hot oven for between 5 and 10 minutes.

Charoseth

Age range
Six plus.

Group size
Individuals.

What you need
1 eating apple,
1 dsp sultanas,
chopped almonds,
cinnamon,
sugar.

What to do
Peel and grate the apple finely. Mix all the other ingredients into the grated apple, adding the almonds and cinnamon according to taste, then roll the mixture into balls and sprinkle with sugar.

Coconut pyramids

Age range
Six plus.

Group size
Small groups or individuals with adult help.

What you need
(for about 24 pyramids)
2 eggs,
200g dried coconut,
100g sugar,
the rind and juice
of half a lemon.

What to do
Beat the sugar and the eggs together. Then add the coconut, grated lemon rind and lemon juice, and mix thoroughly.

Shape into pyramids by pressing a small quantity of the mixture into a moist egg-cup. Bake at 375°F/190°C/gas mark 5 for 15 to 20 minutes until lightly browned.

Easter cards and gifts

Parents will particularly appreciate cards made by the children themselves and children will enjoy making and giving them. The ideas in this chapter could be expanded or adapted, so encourage the children to use their imaginations to make cards which are unique and original.

For an extra touch of personality to Easter gifts, children can also make their own containers – baskets, boxes and cartons – and fill them with eggs or sweets.

Mother's Day card

Age range
Five plus.

Group size
Individuals.

What you need
Coloured card,
cake doily,
pictures of flowers
from magazines,
gardening catalogues
or wallpaper,
or cut-out flower shapes.

What to do
One of the nicest things that children can do for their mothers is to make Mother's Day as pleasant as possible. Remember that some of the very best presents are things you do for people. Encourage the children to give some of their spare time to their mother and help them as much as possible. This Mother's Day card will make the day particularly special.

Take a circle of coloured card and stick on the back of it a larger circle of cake doily. The flower decoration can be cut from gardening catalogues, magazines or wallpaper, or they can be simple flower shapes cut and curved.

The addition of a piece of ribbon tied in a bow to the front of the card and another to make a hanging loop at the top completes the effect. There is space for the message on the back.

Alternatively, a collage of natural seeds, dried or pressed flowers can be used instead of the paper flowers and leaves.

Pressed flower card

Age range
Seven plus.

Group size
Individuals.

What you need
Two colours of card (green and yellow), pressed spring flowers, glue.

What to do
Cut a rectangle of card and fold it in half. Cut an oval shape and stick it on to the front of the card. Glue the pressed flowers on to the oval shape.

Easter card

Age range
Five plus — with help.

Group size
Small groups or individuals.

What you need
Sheet of card, felt-tipped pens, crayons.

What to do
Fold the sheet of card so that the edges overlap. Draw and cut out an egg shape on the folded front. Make sure you do not cut all the way around the egg shape or the front two pieces will fall off.

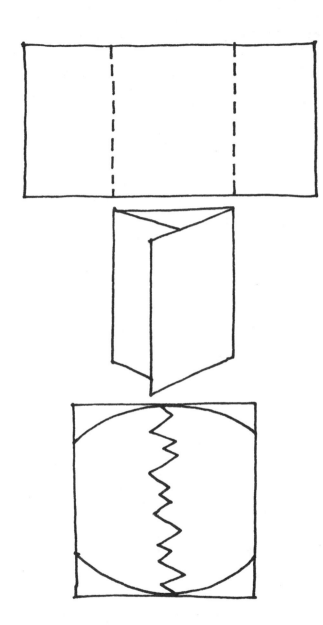

On the inside either draw or paint an Easter chick and write a message.

Cotton-wool card

Age range
Five plus.

Group size
Individuals.

What you need
Card,
balls of coloured
cotton wool,
gummed paper.

What to do
Fold the card in half and on the front stick coloured balls of cotton wool in the shape of a chick or Easter bunny. The features can be cut from coloured card or gummed paper and these can then be glued in place.

Easter bunny card

Age range
Six plus.

Group size
Individuals.

What you need
Cartridge paper or activity paper, white tissue-paper, felt-tipped pens, paints, glue, scissors.

What to do
Cut a rectangle of cartridge paper or activity paper about 25 cm × 10 cm and fold it in half. Draw the shape of a grassy bank on it and cut around the top of the card from A to B (see diagram). Draw the hole on the front of

the card and cut out the shaded part. Write the words 'Happy Easter' along the bottom. Colour the front of the card green to represent grass, then stick tissue-paper

flowers or flowers cut out from magazines around the entrance to the hole. Open it up and trace the Easter Bunny. Colour the background in a dark colour and the

bunny grey with pink ears. When the card is closed, the bunny will peep from his hole. The message can be written on the back.

50

Easter egg card

Age range
Five plus.

Group size
Individuals.

What you need
Card or thick paper,
crêpe paper, paints,
felt-tipped pens or crayons.

What to do
Fold a sheet of card in half and cut out an egg shape as
described previously, taking care not to cut along the

fold. Once it has been cut out, the front of the egg shape
may be decorated by speckling the paint on to it with a
toothbrush, or patterns may be made with crayon in an
all-over pattern or wax resist. When thoroughly dry, take
a strip of crêpe paper about 3½ cm wide and long
enough to go around the egg and glue this across the
middle of the egg. The message may be written inside
and the crêpe paper tied in a bow.

Stand-up card

Age range
Five plus.

Group size
Individuals.

What you need
Card, coloured paper,
crayons, felt-tipped pens,
paints, glue.

What to do
Get the children to draw and cut out a design of a rabbit,
an egg or a chicken and paint or decorate it. This should
then be stuck on to a piece of stiff card and folded as
shown, so that part of the design sticks up above the fold.

Easter bonnet card

Age range
Five plus.

Group size
Individuals.

What you need
Brightly coloured activity paper,
paper doily, tissue-paper scraps,
strips of tissue or crêpe paper,
glue, scissors.

What to do
Fold a sheet of activity paper and cut out a circular shape leaving one side joined. Take the doily and cut out the centre. The outer ring of the doily is then stuck on to the circular card, and the central space filled with tissue balls. The centre of the doily is then stuck over the top of the tissue balls to make the crown of the hat. Finish off

with two strips of crêpe or tissue-paper to hang down, attached at the fold of the card. The message can be written inside and the hat is lifted up by its brim to reveal it.

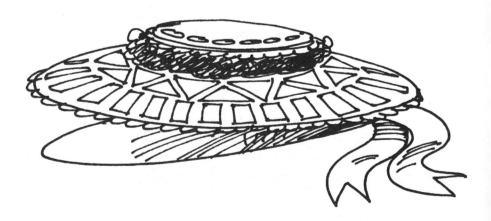

Easter bonnet photomontage

Age range
All ages.

Group size
Individuals.

What you need
Card, crayons, felt-tipped pens, glue, old gardening magazines or seed catalogues.

What to do
Ask the children to draw a picture of themselves (head and shoulders) and colour it in. Stick the picture on to a folded card which is at least half as big again as the picture. Next, cut out flowers from the magazines and stick them on to the drawings as though they are an Easter bonnet. An alternative to this is to decorate an Easter basket. The message can be written on the back.

Quilling

Age range
Seven plus.

Group size
Individuals.

What you need
Strips of coloured activity paper, card, glue, scissors, pencil.

What to do
The strips of quilling should be between 3mm to 25mm wide – any wider than this and the shapes will tend to collapse. To begin any coil, take the end of a strip of paper and wind it around a pencil. Remove the pencil and wind the paper as tight as possible. When you let go the coil should be formed. This will be a loose open coil.

To make an open heart shape, take a strip of paper and fold it in the middle. Wind each end of the strip towards the centre; the coils are allowed to spring apart and left unglued where they touch. These two basic quilling shapes are all that is needed to make this card.

Chick box

Age range
Seven plus.

Group size
Individuals.

What you need
Template (see page 106),
card, crayons or paints,
felt-tipped pens, scissors.

What to do
Trace the template on to a piece of thin card, colour it
with paints or wax crayons.

Cut out the chick and the box taking care to cut on the
thick lines of the front and back curves of the chick and
the solid lines at E and F. The dotted lines are all folded.
Start by folding line A–B to the back or under the chick.
Fold up E–F to make a box. Stick C square over E and D
square over F. Stick the triangular pieces A and B to the
back of the chick to complete the box. This can then be
lined with tissue to make a nest for a chocolate egg or
handful of sweets.

Posy basket

Age range
Six plus.

Group size
Individuals.

What you need
Plastic cap from a spray can or
bottom cut from a plastic bottle,
glue, 2 small doilies.

What to do
Fold a small doily in half and glue it around the cap.

For the handle, get a thin strip of card and glue the
ends inside the cap. Cut a strip of coloured paper or
ribbon and glue it to fit round the bottom of the basket.
Make a small paper or ribbon bow and glue it to the front
of the basket. Cut out a flower from the second doily and
glue it to the centre of the bow.

Cone basket

Age range
Six plus.

Group size
Individuals.

What you need
Circle of card, doily, ribbon, scissors.

What to do
Form the card into a cone. For younger children a template for use as a guide is a good idea (see page 107).

To decorate, take a doily smaller than the basket and glue it to the outside in the same way. Cut a length of ribbon and tie a box in it leaving long ends.

Cut a flower from a doily and staple both the flower and the bow to the centre of the handle. Staple the ends of the handle to the edge of the basket.

Swan

Age range
Six plus.

Group size
Individuals.

What you need
Template of a swan (see page 108), card, pencil, scissors, glue, crêpe paper, felt-tipped pens.

What to do
Using the swan template, draw the outline of two swans on the card and cut them out. Stick the two swan outlines together at the head and neck and along the front edge and back leaving an opening at the top and bottom.

When the glue is thoroughly dry, prise the two swan sections apart in the middle. Cut an oval base with tabs from card and glue it in place securing the tabs to the inside of the swan.

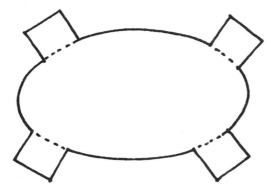

Cut feathers from crêpe paper and glue them on to the swan, working from the back to the front, overlapping them. Feathers could also be made from cut and curled paper and glued into place. Draw on eyes and a beak. An Easter egg may be placed in the middle of the swan's back.

Chicken in a basket

Age range
Seven plus.

Group size
Individuals or small groups.

What you need
Sugar-paper, glue, paints
or felt-tipped pens,
gift ribbon, small doily.

What to do
Take an oblong sheet of sugar-paper and fold it into 16 sections as shown. Curve the corners and cut into them on the long side.

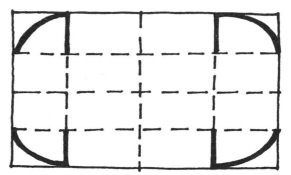

Fold the basket sides up, tuck in the corners, and glue them in place.

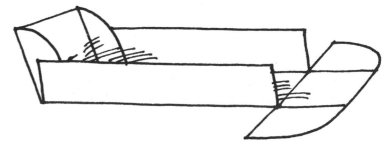

Cut out a chicken shape and add details with felt-tipped pens, paint, crayons or tissue-paper collage.

Glue the chicken to the inside of one side of the basket. Line the basket with straw packing or shredded paper and put in a few chocolate eggs. Attach a handle and decorate the basket with ribbon bows or pieces of doily.

Bucket

Age range
Seven to eight plus.

Group size
Small groups.

What you need
Foldable card, wire, ruler, paper-fasteners.

What to do
Cut and mark an oblong of card as shown. Fold up and glue the overlaps. Make a wire handle and attach it as shown:

Miniature versions can be made into a mobile.

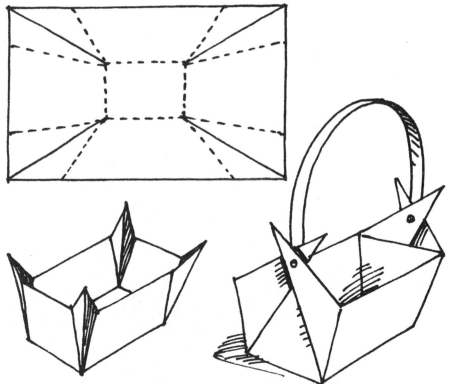

57

Basket

Age range
Six plus.

Group size
Small groups or individuals.

What you need
Rectangle of paper, scissors, stapler.

What to do
Cut a rectangle of paper as shown. Bring the strips

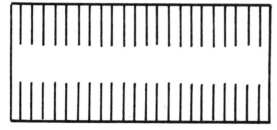

together on each side and hold them with staples, which can be covered with a semicircle of paper before attaching the handle.

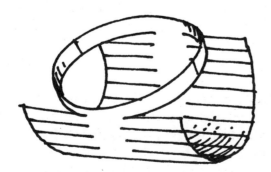

Papier mâché eggs

Age range
Seven plus.

Group size
Pairs or small groups.

What you need
Balloon, scissors, wallpaper paste, paper paints, varnish, strip of lace or doily.

What to do
Blow up the balloon and cover it with papier mâché. Let it dry out thoroughly, then cut the shape in half. Now paint and varnish the egg.

Stick the strip of lace around the edge of the two halves and, when dry, put Easter presents inside.

Easter bunny parcel

Age range
Five plus.

Group size
Individuals.

What you need
Brown fabric, elastic band,
thin brown card,
lollipop stick,
gummed paper, glue.

What to do
Cut out a large brown circle from the brown fabric, and place the chocolate Easter egg or sweets in the centre. Gather the fabric around it and fasten with an elastic band.

Cut a piece of brown card and decorate it to make a rabbit's face. Cut two long ears and glue them to the back of the head. Glue a lollipop stick to the back of the head shape.

Push the lollipop stick through the neck of the bundle to make the rabbit.

Easter egg wrapping paper

Age range
Five plus.

Group size
Small groups
or whole class.

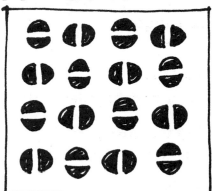

What you need
An egg-sized potato for each child,
sheets of white paper about 30 cm × 45 cm,
a blunt kitchen knife,
a board for cutting, newspaper,
masking tape, PVA or poster paint
in two colours, a tile or an old plate,
card scraps, a sponge to wipe up spilled paint.

What to do
Get the children to fold the paper repeatedly in half until they have a rectangle slightly larger than the potato.

Cut the potato through the middle and place the halves face down on a piece of newspaper. Cut a simple pattern of straight lines or zigzags into the potato.

Stick the unfolded paper to the working surface with masking tape.

Put a blob of paint on to a tile or plate and spread it around with a scrap of card. Take one of the potato halves and rub it face down in the paint, then take it out of the paint and make a print on the paper.

The children can experiment by varying the colour used, and also by inventing different designs.

Easter decorations

Flowers, eggs, rabbits, chicks or a complete Easter meadow will create a springtime atmosphere in the classroom or at home. The decorations in this chapter can be used to hang on an Easter tree, to add to a classroom display or as a table setting for an Easter meal at home. The mobiles will look particularly attractive hung from the ceiling of your classroom. For all the decorations encourage the children to develop their own ideas and adapt the activities described here.

Mexican God's eye

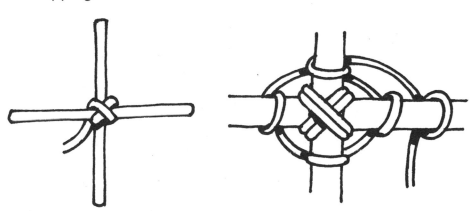

Age range
Seven plus.

Group size
Individuals.

What you need
Coloured yarns and textured threads, fine dowelling or newspaper spills, scissors, double-sided sticky tape.

What to do
Glue two sticks together at right angles and put two strips of double-sided sticky tape across one side of the sticks, stopping short at the ends.

Use the first piece of wool to criss-cross the join in the centre and begin wrapping as shown:

Lay the threads close together so that they overlap each other slightly. Colours can be changed by sticking the ends to one arm and covering them with the next thread.

Pecking birds

Age range
Six plus.

Group size
Individuals.

What you need
Stiff card,
paper-fasteners,
felt-tipped pens, crayons.

Cut two shapes

What to do
Copy or trace the diagrams on to card, cut round the outlines to make two copies and then colour the pieces.

Curled paper crests and feathers may be added.

Push paper-fasteners through from the front of the toy where marked and assemble as in the illustration. When the levers are pulled, the birds move back and forth as if pecking the ground.

cut two shapes

Rabbit with ears that grow

Age range
Five plus.

Group size
Individuals.

What you need
Four fresh carrot tops,
an empty tin can,
a piece of white paper
to cover the tin can,
enough small stones
almost to fill the tin can,
paints, glue, water.

What to do
Cover the tin can with the white paper and decorate it
with a rabbit's face. Put the small stones in the tin and fill
it with water.

Put two carrot tops on one side of the tin and two more
on the other side. Hold the base of each carrot down with
stones and the ears will grow if you keep them well
watered.

Easter tree

Age range
Seven plus.

Group size
Small groups.

What you need
Decorated eggs (see pages 18 to 35),
a twig or small branch of tree.

What to do
Stick the branch into a solid base of Plasticine or put it
into a vase of spring flowers and hang the eggs from the
branches.

Table centre

Age range
Seven plus.

Group size
Small groups.

What you need
A piece of tree bark,
a large and a small decorated Easter egg,
a deep bottle-cap or aerosol lid
covered with silver paper,
short stemmed flowers,
Plasticine or modelling clay.

What to do
Use the Plasticine to fix the bottle-cap and the Easter eggs
to the end of the tree bark. Put water in the bottle-cap and
fill it with flowers.

Rabbit table decoration

Age range
Seven plus.

Group size
Small groups or pairs.

What you need
Doily, glue, paint,
yoghurt carton, sand or soil,
dowelling or knitting needle,
goose egg, ribbon and elastic band.

What to do
Paint the eggshell and stick on ears to represent the
rabbit. Take the knitting needle and put glue on the end.
Place the egg on top and glue it in position.

Stick the yoghurt pot on to the centre of the doily.
Spread the glue around the sides of the yoghurt pot and
pull up the doily. Secure it with an elastic band and turn
the edges of the doily so that they are at right angles to
the rim. Fill the pot with soil or sand and stick the egg and
pole into the centre. Finish off with a ribbon bow.

64

Easter bunny

Age range
Five plus.

Group size
Individuals.

What you need
Cardboard tube, egg carton, card, glue, cotton wool.

What to do
Cut out the ears, arms and legs from the card and one of the sections of the egg carton. Glue this in position for the face. Then glue on the arms, legs and ears. Paint the bunny's features and stick on a piece of cotton wool for the tail.

Make the carrot from a roll of orange paper and another section of the egg carton. Colour the carton section green and stick it to the roll of orange paper. Then glue the carrot into the rabbit's paws.

Woolly lamb

Age range
Five plus.

Group size
Individuals.

What you need
Thin card or stiff cartridge paper, paints, crayons, or felt-tipped pens, fur fabric, sheep's wool, cotton wool or knitting wool.

What to do
For a very simple standing, 2D animal, fold the card or cartridge paper in two and on one side of the paper draw the shape of the trunk, legs and tail.

Place the top of the back on the fold. Draw the head and neck and cut them from a single thickness of card. Colour and mark in the features, then stick the head on to the body. Cover the back with fur, sheep's wool, knitting wool, or cotton wool.

An Easter garden

Age range
Seven plus.

Group size
Pairs or small groups.

What you need
Shallow dish,
potting compost or soil,
3 small wooden crosses
(made from lollipop sticks),
stone, moss, gravel,
seasonal flowers.

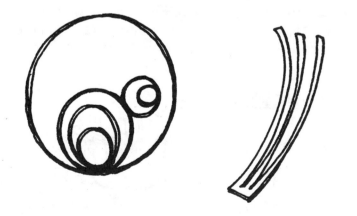

What to do
Line a shallow dish with garden soil or potting compost, and cover it with moss. Make a hollow at the front of the dish and place the stone to the side – this is to represent Christ's tomb. Lay a gravel path around the entrance.

On top of the mound place the three crosses and make a space for a small container for seasonal flowers. Spray the moss with water to keep it fresh.

Chick in an egg

Age range
Six plus.

Group size
Individuals.

What you need
Different-coloured strips of
card about 2 cm wide and
in varying lengths.

What to do
Take a long strip of card about 40 cm long and make an oval shape. Then make three circles for the body – one large, one medium, one small. For the head make one medium and one small circle. Glue them together as shown in the illustration.

Then cut out a beak in a contrasting colour and a tail which is just one strip cut lengthwise. Stick them to the body to finish the chick.

Chicken mobiles

Age range
Five plus.

Group size
Individuals.

What you need
Yellow tissue-paper,
black, yellow and orange card,
black felt-tipped pen.

What to do
Cut out two circles of card, one for the body and one for the head, cut out two legs and feet from the orange card; assemble the chick as shown in the diagram.

Glue on a triangle for the tail and cut out small triangles for the beak. Draw the eye using a black felt-tipped pen. Feathers can be cut out from the yellow tissue-paper and stuck on the side for the wings.

Another chicken mobile can be made simply using one circle. The eyes are cut from white card and the beak is a diamond shape folded in half and slotted into a cut on the circle. The tail is a fan shape stuck on the opposite side and the legs are a strip of card about 4 cm × 9 cm folded into a triangle. A slit is cut into the top of the triangle and the body of the bird slots in. They can be hung as mobiles or quite easily stood in a group.

Bird in a hoop

Age range
Seven plus.

Group size
Individuals.

What you need
Two large sheets of paper, a bird template (see page 109), a pair of compasses, a pencil, scissors, felt-tipped pens or paints, sequins, glue.

What to do
Fold one sheet of paper in half. Use the template or draw the outline of the bird on the paper, making sure that the bird's back is placed along the folded edge.

Cut out the bird. Draw the outline of the wings on the cut-out bird and colour the feathers. Glue the sequins in place to represent eyes. Cut out the shaped edges of the wings through both thicknesses of paper, leaving the edge nearest the bird's head attached. Fold the wings back to make it look as if the bird is flying.

Fold the second piece of paper in half and draw a heart with one of its straight edges against the fold. Use the pair of compasses to draw a circle in the position indicated. Cut out the heart-shaped hoop and then cut the circle from the heart. Decorate the heart-shaped hoop to represent the bird's perch.

Cut a slit from the circle towards the point of the heart. Do not cut through the hoop. Cut a slit in the front of the bird and slot it in position on the hoop. Be careful where you make this cut as it will affect the bird's centre of gravity and the way it sits on its perch.

Easter egg mobiles

Age range
Five plus.

Group size
Individuals.

What you need
Card, paints, decorations, scissors, a sharp knife, a toothbrush.

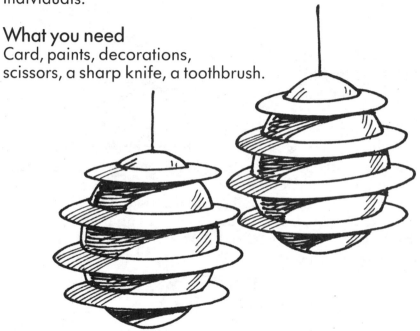

What to do
These are easily made from card which has been decorated by using the splattering technique with an old toothbrush.

Cut out one large egg shape and then cut out oval shapes of varying sizes. But cutting a slit with a sharp knife, these ovals can be slipped on to the large egg to produce a 3D Easter egg which can be hung in groups around the classroom.

Humpty Dumpty mobile

Age range
Five plus.

Group size
Individuals.

What you need
Card, paints, glue, felt-tipped pens,
cartridge paper, wool.

What to do
Cut out an oval shape from the card and draw or paint a
face on the top half. Decorate the lower half in the form
of clothes and stick on concertina arms and legs.

Expanding hare

Age range
Six plus.

Group size
Individuals.

What you need
Paper, coloured paper
scraps, glue,
cotton wool, thread.

What to do
Take a rectangle of paper and fold and cut it as shown.

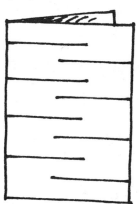

Add the hare's face and paws. Perhaps he could be
holding an Easter egg.

Experiment with bodies of various sizes and hang it
from the ceiling with thread or a thin strip of crêpe paper.

A Chinese lantern

Age range
Seven plus.

Group size
Individuals.

What you need
Coloured paper, tissue or
crêpe paper (optional),
glue, scissors, string.

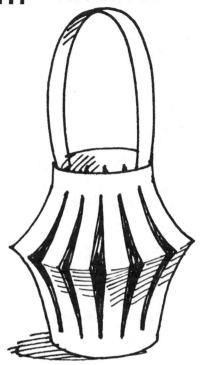

Open the paper and hold it so that the scissor cuts are
vertical, form the paper into a cylindrical shape and glue
the edges together. Then take a strip of coloured paper
2 cm × 30 cm and glue it into position at the top of the
lantern to make a handle.

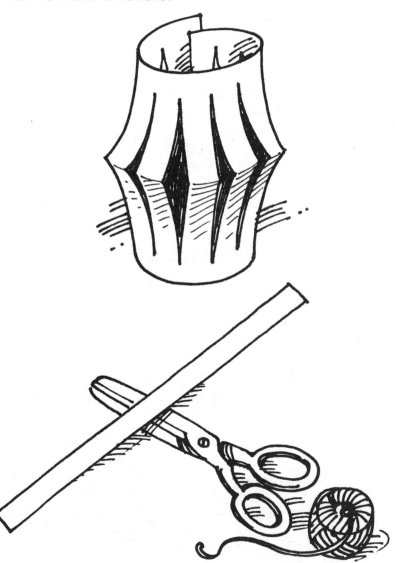

What to do
Take a rectangle of coloured paper, about 30 cm × 20
cm and fold it in half to make a rectangle 30 cm × 10 cm.
Cut the rectangle from the folded side to a depth of 8 cm
as shown.

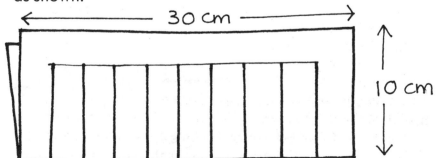

Alternatively, use a strip of card 4 cm × 60 cm, formed into a circle with strips of tissue or crêpe paper hung from it as shown.

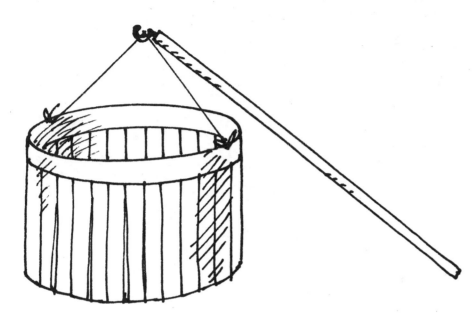

Thread string through the card so that the lantern can be hung from a stick or pole.

Chinese fish

Age range
Seven plus.

Group size
Small groups or individuals.

What you need
A variety of different-coloured tissue-paper, scissors, PVA glue, florist's wire, string, a stick or a pole.

What to do
Cut out two fish shapes from tissue-paper and then overlay them with different-coloured tissue-paper to create the eyes and fins. Coat the two sides with PVC glue to give them strength and then glue them together all round the edge.

Insert an oval of florist's wire into the mouth of the fish and glue the two halves of the fish's mouth to this. This will give the fish more of a 3D shape. The string can be threaded through the dorsal fin and attached to a stick or a pole.

Easter bonnets and masks

On the afternoon of Easter Day, springtime is celebrated and people traditionally wear new clothes to mark the change of the seasons. In Victorian times, people would stroll up and down the roads to see and be seen. Sometimes Easter parades are held on Easter Day, including competitions for the best Easter bonnet. Here are a few ideas for children to make their own Easter bonnets. Perhaps you could hold a competition of your own.

Many countries have carnivals and processions on Easter Day and throughout Holy Week. Exotic masks lend themselves to a carnival atmosphere. A basic mask shape can be decorated with seeds or pasta and sprayed with gold paint. The decoration can be anything which will make the mask colourful and interesting.

If the masks are to be held they could be attached to sticks and held to the face.

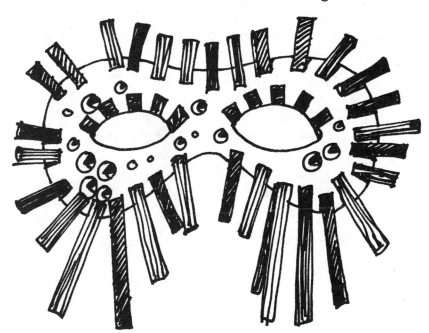

A more elaborate basic shape can be painted and feathers and sequins added.

Beaks and noses for the masks can be made from triangles or diamond shapes of card or paper, folded down the middle and stuck in place.

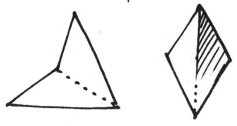

73

Papier mâché hats

Age range
Seven plus.

Group size
Individuals.

What you need
Balloon,
paper,
cold water paste.

What to do
Cover the balloon with pieces of paper and glue for about ten layers. When it is dry, pop the balloon and cut the shape you want. Cut lengthways, you will have a shape like the one shown below:

This shape can be made into all sorts of creatures, or simply decorated with flowers, Easter eggs, chicks or rabbits.

It could be made into a ladybird with black spots, a butterfly with wings framed with wire and covered with tissue-paper. For a mouse, add card or felt ears, string stiffened with glue for the whiskers, buttons for the eyes and twisted wool for the tail.

If the papier mâché shape is cut horizontally, the shape makes a pixie hat or a helmet according to the decoration.

Top hat

Age range
Seven plus.

Group size
Individuals.

What you need
Card,
tape,
glue,
scissors.

What to do
Make the card into a cylinder to fit your head. Fix the side and cut flaps at the top and bottom – these should be about 5 cm deep.

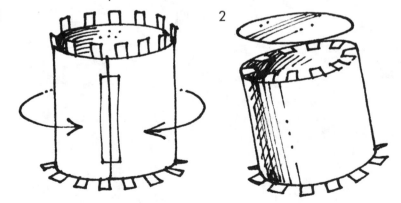

To make a brim, cut a hole using the cylinder as a template to get the correct size. Cut a top for the hat, again use the cylinder as a template and fix the top on with glue.

The brim may be decorated with flowers or feathers, or curls of coloured paper and Cellophane.

Bonnet

Age range
Five plus.

Group size
Individuals.

What you need
Card,
stapler,
glue,
paper flowers,
doilies,
feathers or
any other
suitable decoration.

What to do

Cut out the shape as shown in the diagram, bearing in mind the distance between stapling points is the depth of the back of the hat. Attach a ribbon to the front section to tie under the child's chin. Staple firmly at the points marked and decorate as you wish.

Cone hat

Age range
Five plus.

Group size
Individuals.

What you need
Card, stapler, coloured or plain decorations as required.

What to do

Draw a circle and cut out a triangle as shown in the diagram. Staple them together and decorate as appropriate.

Decorations can be made from cartridge paper or tissue-paper for the hats.

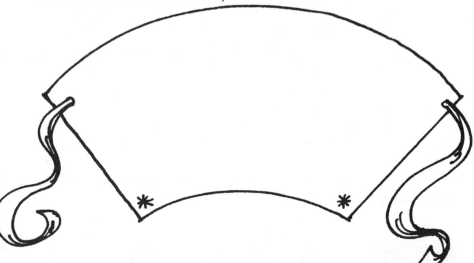

75

Headbands

Age range
Five plus.

Group size
Individuals.

What you need
Stong card,
glue,
paper for cut-outs,
felt-tipped pens,
beads or buttons
for decoration.

What to do
Cut the headband to
fit the child's head and
decorate with felt-tipped
pens, crayons, painted
cut-outs or buttons etc.

Simple band with streamers

Age range
Five plus.

Group size
Individuals.

What you need
Card,
tissue,
glue,
scissors.

What to do
Cut a strip of card to fit over the top of the head and make
some simple tissue-paper flowers to stick on. Cut some
strips of tissue-paper to hang down on either side of the
head.

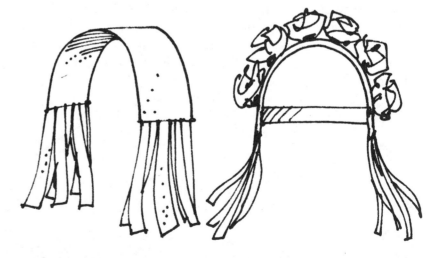

A strip of card can be attached at the back to keep the
headband in place.

Floral headband

Age range
Five plus.

Group size
Individuals.

What you need
Tissue-paper flowers,
large paper bow,
glue,
strip of strong card.

What to do
Make the headband to fit the child's head (see page 76).
Decorate it with flowers and add a large paper bow at
the back.

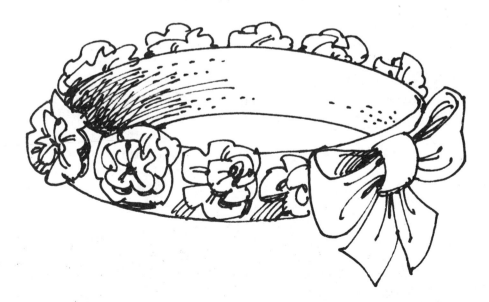

Cone-shaped hats

Age range
Five plus.

Group size
Individuals.

What you need
Card,
stapler,
glue,
scissors,
scarves,
pompons,
decorations.

What to do
Cut out circles of strong card. Remove a triangle as
shown in the diagram and fold it to make a cone. Secure
it firmly.

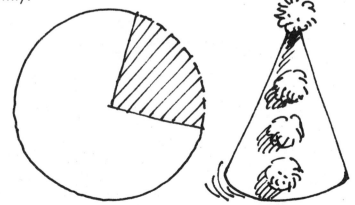

For a clown's hat add a row of pompons.
For a witch or wizard's hat, add a brim and decorate it
extravagantly.

77

Wide-brimmed hat

Age range
Five plus.

Group size
Individuals.

What you need
Tissue-paper,
crêpe paper,
card,
glue,
scissors.

What to do
Cut a large and a small circle of card. Place the smaller circle in the centre of the large circle and draw round it. Fill the circle with crushed tissue-paper and glue the small circle on top. Finish off with a long crêpe paper ribbon attached at both sides of the large circle.

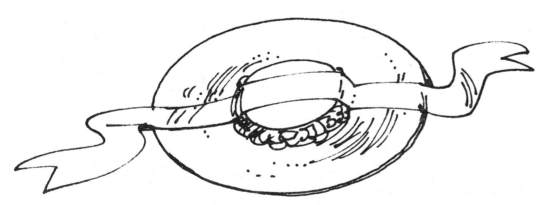

Doily Easter bonnet

Age range
Five plus.

Group size
Individuals.

What you need
A paper doily 10 cm diameter
or a circle of paper cut to
achieve a similar lacey effect,
a circle of thin card in contrasting
colour – large enough to fit the head,
ribbon or wool,
odds and ends
of tissue-paper,
foil, Cellophane,
clear glue.

What to do
Make tissue-paper flowers by folding small squares into four and twisting them to make a stem. Poke the stems of the flowers through the doilies, stick them down firmly on the wrong side and leave them to dry. Cut two lengths of ribbon or wool long enough to tie around the chin and fix to either side of the card circle. Stick the decorated doily on top of the circle to complete the hat. Add a few more decorations of your choice for extra effect.

Rabbit mask

Age range
Six plus.

Group size
Individuals.

What you need
Card,
paints,
felt-tipped pens,
strips of wool,
gummed paper,
stapler or glue.

What to do
Cut out from the card the two main shapes for the face as shown in the diagram. Fold a sheet of card in two, draw the ears and cut them out.

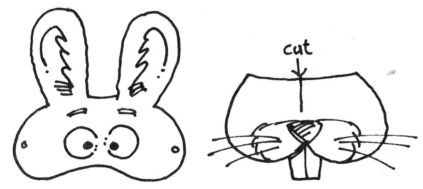

Cut from the top of the lower part of the mask, overlap the two pieces, and staple them together. Then staple on the upper part of the mask, and glue or staple on the ears. Add the features using either cut-out shapes from gummed paper or felt-tipped pens.

Chicken mask

Age range
Six plus.

Group size
Individuals.

What you need
Card,
paints,
felt-tipped pens,
strips of wool,
gummed paper,
stapler or glue.

What to do
The mask is made in the same way as the rabbit mask (see page 79); just the two component parts are different.

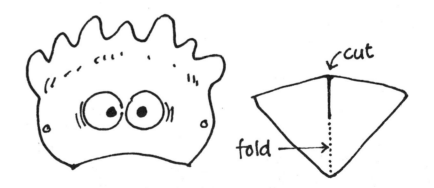

Cut and overlap the lower part which makes the beak, and attach it to the upper part with staples. Cut the eyes from gummed paper or colour with paints or felt-tipped pens. Finally fold the lower part of the beak.

Nature at Easter

Easter was originally a spring festival and at this time of year many countries celebrate spring in their own way. It is an ideal time for children to learn about animals and plants as they begin to grow and blossom.

You could encourage the children to make a list of the differences they observe as the season changes from late January until late April or early May – young animals being born, birds building nests and laying eggs, butterflies emerging, animals coming out of hibernation, frog and toad spawn changing into tadpoles, and so on.

Looking at trees

Age range
Five plus.

Group size
Small groups.

What you need
A variety of branches, access to a variety of trees.

What to do
Give the children a variety of branches to look at and encourage them to observe the differences.

Carefully cut a bud lengthwise to show all the leaves packed tightly inside. Put the twigs in water on a sunny window-sill so that the children can observe the leaves emerging day by day.

If the children have access to a variety of trees they will notice that they do not all come out at the same time, and they could keep a record of when the first buds began to open.

81

Bird-spotting

Age range
Seven plus.

Group size
Small groups.

What you need
Bird-spotting books.

What to do
This is the time when birds choose a mate and begin to nest. With the aid of bird-spotting books or manuals, children can spot and identify birds from their plumage, their shape in flight, or their song.

Feeding birds

Age range
Six plus.

Group size
Small groups.

What you need
Bird food, such as bits of bacon and cheese rind, bread, peanuts in mesh bags, over-ripe apples, dried fruit such as sultanas and raisins.

What to do
Children can make birds welcome by providing food, such as bits of bacon and cheese rind. Peanuts in mesh bags can be purchased (remember that salted peanuts are not good for birds). Over-ripe apples and dried fruit, such as sultanas and raisins, are also a good idea.

The children could design a feeding table, bearing in mind that the food should be off the ground to guard against predators and to discourage vermin. The table should have raised edges to keep the food in place, and could have compartments for different types of food, including a place for a container of water.

Put a variety of foods on the table, and the children can make a chart (see page 110) to show which birds like which foods.

Younger children could simply observe which are the most popular foods among all the birds which visit the table.

Nest-building

Age range
Seven plus.

Group size
Small groups.

What you need
Plastic gloves,
cotton wool,
wool or string,
paper, feathers,
straw (or 12½ mm thick plywood
and tools to make nesting box).

What to do
If you can find any old nests the children could examine
how the nests have been constructed. Make sure they *are*
old nests, and be careful not to disturb ones which are
still in use. Either the children must wear plastic gloves, or

the nests should be baked in an oven to kill any germs or
tiny insects. During the examination, stress how long it
will have taken the birds to build the nests, and that
birds' nests and eggs must be left alone during
springtime.

The children could collect the materials they discover in
the old nests and try to build their own.

Some of the nesting materials could be attached to a
line so that the children can see which materials are
chosen most often by the birds.

If you prefer, you could make a nesting box from
12½ mm thick plywood. To encourage blue tits, make the
entry hole quite small; if it is made a little larger, house
sparrows may nest in it. The box should be fastened to a
tree or wall about 2 m from the ground, out of the reach
of cats.

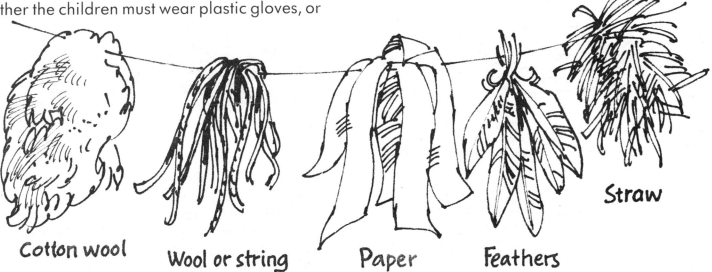

Cotton wool   Wool or string   Paper   Feathers   Straw

A bird bath

Age range
Seven plus.

Group size
Small groups.

What you need
Dustbin liners, gravel.

What to do
A bird bath is easily made by digging a hole about 15 cm deep and about 1 m across. Line this with a dustbin liner held in place by large stones all around the edge. A little gravel sprinkled on the bottom and a perch in the middle will encourage the birds to bathe or drink from the bath.

Looking at mini-beasts

Age range
Eight plus.

Group size
Small groups.

What you need
Jam jar, soil, coloured sand, brown paper, sweet crumbs or sugar, sheet of perspex, plastic bricks, small paintbrush, plastic pot with cloth cover, cardboard box, plant spray.

What to do
On a warm day, get the children to go outside and lift up stones carefully to see what is underneath. They may be surprised at the variety of creatures – worms, woodlice, beetles, spiders, slugs, snails. Make sure the children replace the stones very carefully so as not to destroy the miniature world below.

Begin by studying earthworms — these will be a lot easier to find after a shower of rain or in light soil. Let the children dig for worms themselves so that they can see the variety of shapes and sizes. Encourage them to observe the way the worms move on stiff paper and then in soil; they will see how the worms feel about in the soil until they find a gap to wriggle down into. The children could then draw their worms.

Explain that worms are welcomed by gardeners and farmers since they mix up the soil, letting air into it. To demonstrate this, fill a jam jar with four alternate layers of soil and coloured sand. Press each layer as level as possible and put a layer of leaves on the top with four or five earthworms. Cover the outside of the jar with brown paper and keep out the light, and keep the soil moist. Put the jar in a cool place, and look at it later to see how the worms have mixed up the soil and sand and dragged the leaves down.

Children may be able to find a nest of ants by dropping some sweet crumbs or sugar on the ground near the ants, and watching them carry the crumbs back to their nest. Encourage the children to observe how the ants move and to compare their scurrying movements with the slow movements of snails.

A couple of snails could be taken into the classroom to enable the children to see how they move, and to observe the silvery trail they leave. To make this observation easier, place a sheet of perspex across four stacks of plastic bricks, as shown.

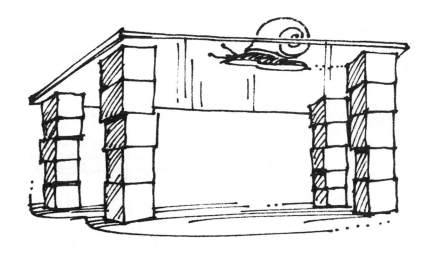

Woodlice can be found under stones, dead wood and leaves. The children could collect some woodlice using a small paintbrush and a plastic pot, and take them into the classroom. Put various natural materials (such as dead leaves, a piece of decaying wood, a little soil and a couple of stones) into a cardboard box, 20 cm × 30 cm × 8 cm, then make some ventilation holes in the lid of the box and spray the contents with water.

The children can then watch the woodlice and attempt to draw them, observing what happens when they are touched gently with the brush. They should be returned to the same place they came from after a few days.

Children might well find other creatures, such as millipedes, centipedes, ants, slugs and spiders. Try to find spiders' webs, too, and see how they sparkle with dew in the early morning sunlight.

Growing seeds

Age range
Seven plus.

Group size
Small groups.

What you need
Four small jars (one with a lid),
cress seeds, cotton wool.

What to do
By varying the conditions, children can find out what their
seeds need to make them grow successfully.

Take four small jars (one with a lid), some cress seeds
and some cotton wool. In the first jar, put the cress seeds
on damp cotton wool and place the jar in a light position.
These seeds will grow because they have moisture, light,
warmth and air.

In the second jar place the seeds on dry cotton wool
and put them next to the first jar. These will not grow
because they have no moisture.

Put damp cotton wool and cress seeds in the third jar,
but place it in the refrigerator. These seeds will not grow
because they are too cold.

In the fourth jar the air must be removed. This can be
done by boiling water, then putting seeds and boiled
water in a jar and screwing the lid on tightly.
Alternatively, put the seeds and water into the jar and
pour cooking oil on to the top of the water as a seal.
These seeds will not grow as they will have no air.

Children can experiment further by varying the soils
and seeds. They could use clay, sand, stones, leaf mould
or a mixture of these, and find out which soil produces the
best results.

Pond life

Age range
Eight plus.

Group size
Whole class with two or three adults to supervise.

What you need
Access to a pond, a large tank, pond weed, fish food, scraps of meat, air pump (optional).

What to do
If there is a pond nearby, take the children pond-dipping to see what kinds of creatures they can find.

Frog or toad spawn can be kept easily in a large tank, so that the children can watch the change from eggs to tadpoles to tiny frogs or toads. It is important that tadpoles have pond weed to cling to and eat when they first emerge. Then give them fish food for the first few weeks, going on to scraps of meat. Make sure that the water does not become stale – an air pump will help.

When the tadpoles have completed their change into baby frogs or toads, a stone or rock placed in the water with the top clear of the surface will enable them to adapt to their amphibious life. As soon as they are fully formed, they must be returned to the pond.

Here are some of the creatures the children may find:

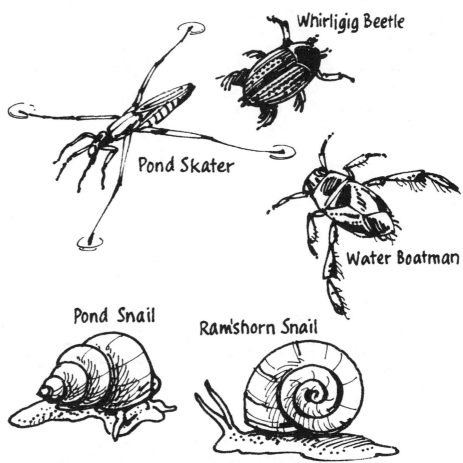

Whirligig Beetle

Pond Skater

Water Boatman

Pond Snail

Ram'shorn Snail

Drops of pond water viewed under a microscope can reveal a fascinating world of aquatic life, and if you are lucky you may be able to get the larvae of dragonflies, watersnails and other creatures.

Measuring rainfall

Age range
Seven plus.

Group size
Small groups.

What you need
A flat-bottomed bottle,
a funnel with the same size
mouth as the bottle bottom.

What to do
Place the funnel inside the bottle and put it securely in an
open place where raindrops cannot splash off other
surfaces. It will soon become apparent that a heavy
shower is needed to produce a couple of centimetres in
the bottom of the jar.

Measuring wind speed

Age range
Eight plus.

Group size
Small groups or whole class.

What you need
Strips of wood,
several strips of tissue-paper.

What to do
Fix several strips of tissue-paper securely to the strips of
wood and put them in an open place. The strength of the
wind is indicated by the angle of the strips of paper.

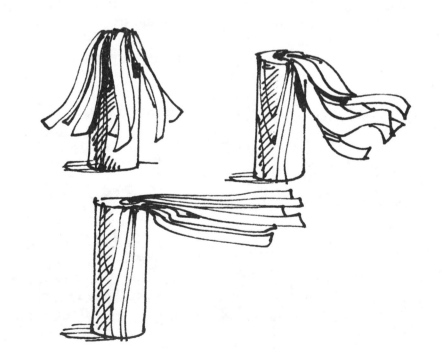

Weather vane

Age range
Seven to eleven.

Group size
Small groups.

What you need
Plastic drinking straw,
scissors, a pin,
a length of wood
(square-sided if possible),
card, glue,
a compass, a plastic bead.

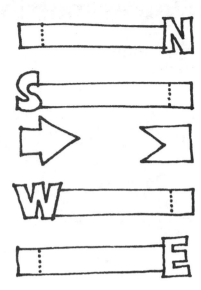

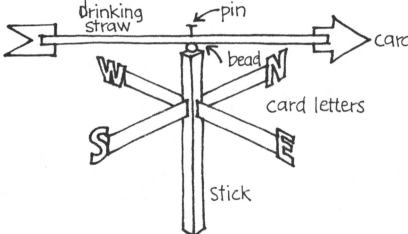

What to do
Cut a 1 cm slit in each end of the straw and push the pin through the centre of the straw. The hole must be large enough for the straw to spin easily. Place a small plastic bead below the straw and stick the pin into the end of the piece of wood (see illustration). This will help the straw to spin freely.

Cut out a pointer and a tail and push them into the slits in the straw. These can be glued in position. From the card, cut out the letters for the points of the compass and glue one to each side of the stick. Use the compass to line up the weather vane and record the wind direction.

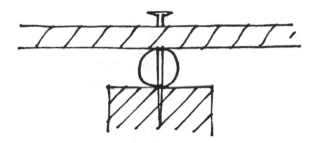

A wind rose could be made to record the wind direction over a period of days. Draw the compass points in boxes on a large sheet of paper. Each day, draw a line across the box or 'petal' to show the direction of the wind that day.

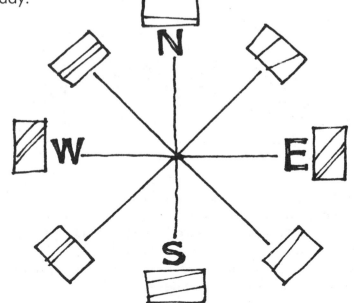

Rainbows

Age range
Eight plus.

Group size
Small groups

What you need
Prisms,
mirrors,
washing-up liquid,
petrol,
a rainbow!

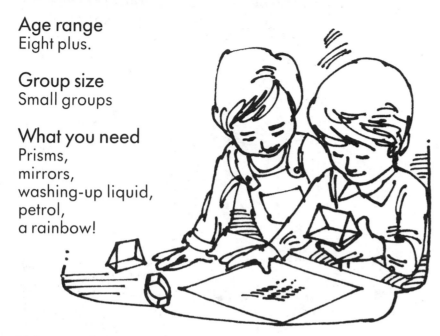

What to do
Rainbows are often seen in spring especially with great variations in weather.

A rainbow is created by the reflection of sunlight from drops of water in the sky and it occurs when the rain is falling opposite the sunshine.

Children can observe the colours of the rainbow, if they use a prism to show the colour spectrum. They may look out for rainbows on soap bubbles, edges of bevelled mirrors, fish skins and sometimes, when there is a puddle in the road, spilled petrol floats on the surface and the rainbow colours swirl and spiral.

There is a legend that there is a pot of gold at the end of the rainbow.

The children can observe that the rainbow moves away as they walk towards it, so it never really ends anywhere.

Flower spotting

Age range
Six plus.

Group size
Small groups or whole class.

What you need
Check-lists
(see pages 111 and 112),
pencils,
guides for wild
and garden flowers.

What to do
Give each child a copy of pages 00 and 00 and let the children suggest the flowers they are likely to see. Leave a few empty columns for any flowers you may come across unexpectedly.

As they see the different species, ask the children to tick the appropriate column. The guides can be used to identify any unknown plants.

Because these flowers do not bloom at the same time, the walks will have to take place at regular intervals over a couple of months and the children will need to make a careful note of the date of their observations.

Flower chart

Age range
Eight plus.

Group size
Whole class.

What you need
Squared paper (see page 113),
coloured pencils.

What to do
Get the children to observe a group of different flowering
plants and put them in the order that they flower. Ask
them to make a chart of their observations using the
squared paper – one square should be coloured in for
each week of flowering. The flowers should be easily
accessible, so that regular observations can take place.

Traditional games and pastimes

Easter begins with Shrovetide and this is the season for traditional games. At one time, the most popular game was football but it is was very different from the game we know today. It was probably introduced by the Romans and it was played in the streets without any rules, and in some cases the goals were about a mile apart or there were no definite goals at all. The pitch might have no set boundaries and sometimes hundreds of players took part in the game, which could last all day.

Pancakes

Pancake races are held in many parts of Britain; the most famous of these is at Olney in Buckinghamshire.

These races are thought to have started when a housewife who was cooking pancakes heard the church bells ring. Thinking she was late for the service she ran off and arrived at the church still holding the pan in her hand. Now each Shrove Tuesday, housewives who live in the area race from the Market Square to the Parish Church. They have to toss the pancakes three times and

are allowed to pick them up if they drop them. The winner receives a kiss and a prayer book from the vicar who says to her, 'The peace of the Lord be always with you.' The verger or bell-ringer gets two rewards: a kiss from the winner and her pancake. Later all the frying pans are taken into the church, and the ladies take part in a short service.

About 30 years ago people of the town of Liberal in Kansas, USA, began to take an interest in the Olney race, and now they too hold a pancake race, competing for the best time to cover the distance.

Many other Shrovetide customs are still practised today. At Westminster School in London, they have the Pancake Greaze every year. Originally the school cook had to toss a pancake over a long iron curtain pole which divided the older boys from the younger boys in the Great Schoolroom. When he did so, all the boys rushed forward to see who could get the pancake. They winner received a guinea from the Dean. Now only one boy from each form competes. Two minutes after the pancake is tossed over the bar 'Time' is called, and the winner is the boy who has managed to hang on to the largest piece of pancake.

Skipping games

Skipping is carried out in many places on Good Friday and perhaps this was a good way of keeping warm on cold spring days. Spring is traditionally the time when children get out their skipping ropes, but this activity was once enjoyed by everybody. It is a very old activity which was supposed to have the magical power to make the seeds grow in the spring and in Brighton the local name for Good Friday was 'Long Rope Day'. Today only a few people gather to skip at the sea front, but Good Friday skipping still exists at Alciston in Sussex outside the Rose Cottage Inn, where sometimes as many as 200 skippers meet.

Marbles

Marbles is a game which was played especially in the north of England, and also in Surrey and Sussex. The 'marble season' began on Ash Wednesday and finished on Good Friday. This last day was once known as Marble Day in the southern counties of England. At Tinsley Green near Crawley in Sussex, a championship match is still held on Good Friday and the custom is thought to have started when two men wanted to marry the same girl. In order to determine who should, they both agreed to play a game of marbles.

No one knows whether either of them married the girl, but the two men met year after year and invited others to join in. Now the contest has grown and people travel from many countries to take part in the World Marbles Championship.

Spinning tops

Spinning tops were very popular on Good Friday and they have a long history that goes back to Ancient Greeks and Romans. The season was from Shrove Tuesday to Good Friday, and children used to play with them during Lent when they would cry:

Tops are in, spin 'em agin,
Tops are out, smuggin' about.

Smuggin' means that the tops could justifiably be taken if they were played with out of season. All toys which were made to spin on a point or a peg were called tops and there are lots of different kinds: whipping, peg, and humming are just a few. The whipping top was the most popular, and in ancient times a dried eel skin was used as a whip, thong or lash.

The lash is wound around the top and is then pulled quickly away. The top is kept spinning by whipping it at intervals. A well-spun top hums and may even stay still in one spot just as if it had gone to sleep, and this is said to be the origin of the saying 'to sleep like a top'.

Easter eggs

Easter eggs are not only eaten and decorated but are also used in a variety of games in different parts of the world. Egg-rolling is one of these, and it is thought to commemorate the rolling away of the stone from Christ's tomb. Coloured eggs were rolled down hills or banks and it meant good luck if your egg remained intact until it reached the bottom. Sometimes there would be a competition to see whose egg rolled the furthest.

In America, egg-rolling has been an annual event for more than 150 years on the lawns of the White House in Washington. Another egg-rolling contest is held in New York's Central Park. Children up to the age of 12 roll wooden eggs with wooden spoons across a lawn. This is a modern custom, and the winners can get toys and cash prizes since there are no cracked edible eggs to serve as prizes. At Preston in Lancashire, the highlight of Easter Monday for all the local children is when they go to Avenham Park to roll eggs down the grassy slopes.

Other games include egg-tapping. Here the egg is held in the clenched fist, and the end is tapped against the

egg of an opponent who holds his egg in the same way. If he manages to break his opponent's egg he may claim it as his own.

Pace-egging was when groups of children went around begging for eggs and other gifts. In return they would perform the Pace Egg Play, an Easter version of the Mummers' Play. The costumes for this consisted simply of sewing paper streamers on to their ordinary clothes, and their faces were blackened by soot or hidden by masks of the characters they were playing. In later years the play was not always presented and the performance was limited to the singing of songs like:

We are two/three jolly boys all of one mind
We are come a-pace-egging and we hope you'll prove kind
We hope you'll prove kind with your eggs and strong beer
And we'll come no more a-pace-egging until another year

In France and some parts of Great Britain eggs were thrown in the air and caught again as they fell. The player who dropped one had to pay a forfeit.

Ball games

Other games played during Easter include 'knur and spell', 'ninepins' and 'tipcat'. A knur is a small, hard, pot ball and a spell is a machine with a spring which sends the ball into the air. The object is to hit the knur as far as possible with a wooden stick as it flies upwards. Tipcat is a similar game played with a shaped piece of wood called a 'cat', and once again the object is to send the 'cat' as far as possible by hitting it with a wooden stick called a catstaff.

Easter Monday is still called 'Ball Monday' in some parts of Oxfordshire, because of the games such as bowls, stoolball, football and handball, played on this day. Ball-games and 'scrambles' go back to pagan times, but no one seems to know why.

Bottle kicking

At Hallaton in Leicestershire there is the traditional Hare Pie Scramble and Bottle Kicking. A hare pie is taken to the church gate in procession from the 'Royal Oak', and on Hare Pie Bank the crowd scramble for pieces of pie which are 'thrown' by the rector. Later on the Bottle Kicking match starts between Hallaton and Medbourne. The prize is a barrel of ale. Although it is called the Bottle Kicking Contest no bottles are used.

There are three barrels in the contest, two full of ale and one empty. One of the full barrels is placed on the top of Hare Pie Bank and that is where the match starts; the two teams have to get the barrels over the opposite touchlines. The Hallaton touchline wins the brook on one

side of the bank and the Medbourne touchline is the hedge on the other de. The team to get the first barrel across the touchline gets the ale inside. While they drink it there is an interval. The empty barrel is then played for in the same way, and whichever team gets this second barrel over their touchline is the overall winner and wins the third barrel which is still full of ale.

Making the crops grow

The custom of 'heaving' or 'lifting' on Easter Monday and Tuesday was once a very popular sport. It started as a magic rite to make crops grow tall. On Easter Monday, groups of young men decorated chairs with evergreen branches and ribbons and then they would carry them around the neighbourhood. Women and girls had to sit in the chairs and they were lifted high in the air three times. They had to pay a forfeit in order to be released. The next day it was the women's turn. In some places the day order was reversed but on both days lifting had to stop at noon.

Water games

Water was also a part of some games at Easter and Easter Monday was sometimes known as 'Ducking Monday' in parts of Eastern Europe.

Young men and girls would splash each other with water. In Hungary unmarried girls would be taken at daybreak to the local pond or stream, and thrown in by the young men. This was supposed to make them good wives in the future. Where there was no pond or stream the girls would be drenched with buckets of water, and they were even expected to pay for this privilege with gifts of painted eggs or glasses of brandy!

It seems they did this willingly, since to be left out implies a lack of popularity and the ducking or splashing is therefore regarded as a real compliment.

Activities

- Ask the children to try to describe a game of marbles.
- Get the children to list all the skipping rhymes they know.
- Make a simple top by pushing a meat skewer through a cotton reel. A thin strip of leather or string attached to a stick can be used as a lash.
- Organise an egg-rolling game to see whose egg rolls the furthest. A simple graph can be made to illustrate this. Don't forget the measuring involved in this activity. The distance covered will depend upon the angle of the slope. The steeper the slope, the longer the distance.
- Find out about the rules of some of the games mentioned. See if you can set up a competition.

Reproducible material

Foreign words for Easter

Pâques
France

Pask
Sweden

Paaske
Denmark

Pasqua
Italy

Paach
Holland

Pascua
Spain

Pasg
Wales

Greetings to copy

Greetings to copy

Template for Easter biscuits, see page 43

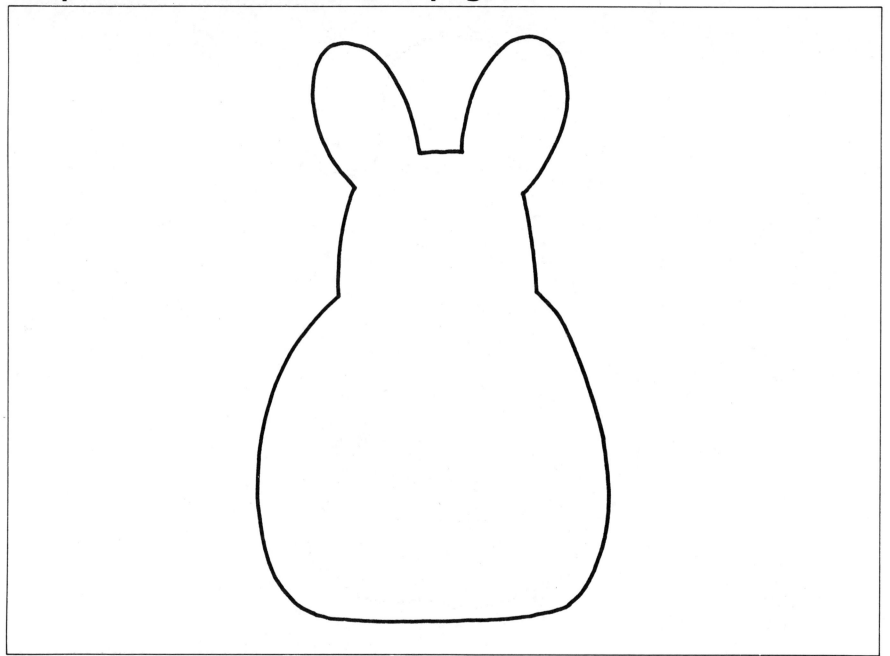

Template for Italian dove cake, see page 44

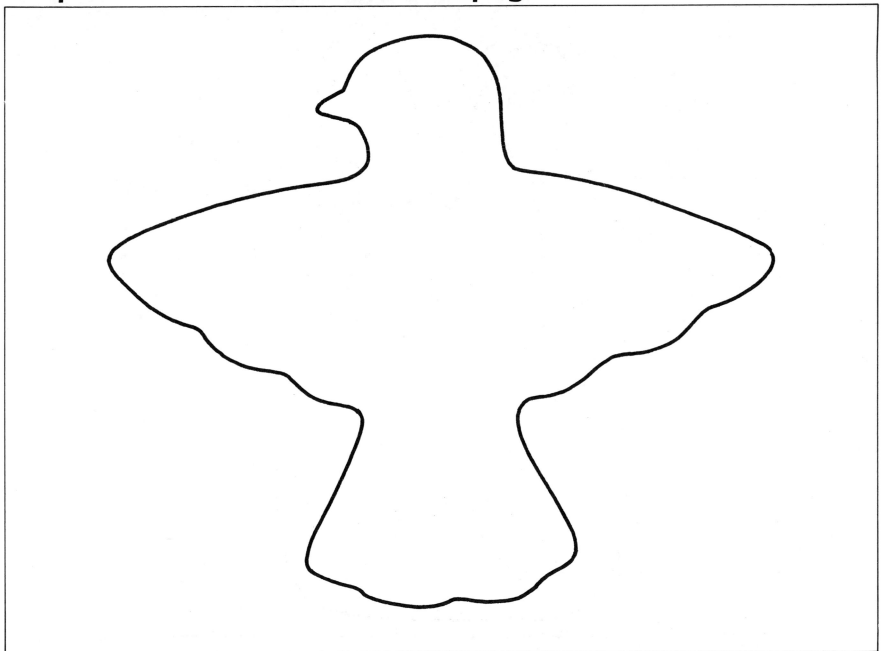

Template for Cane basket, see page 55

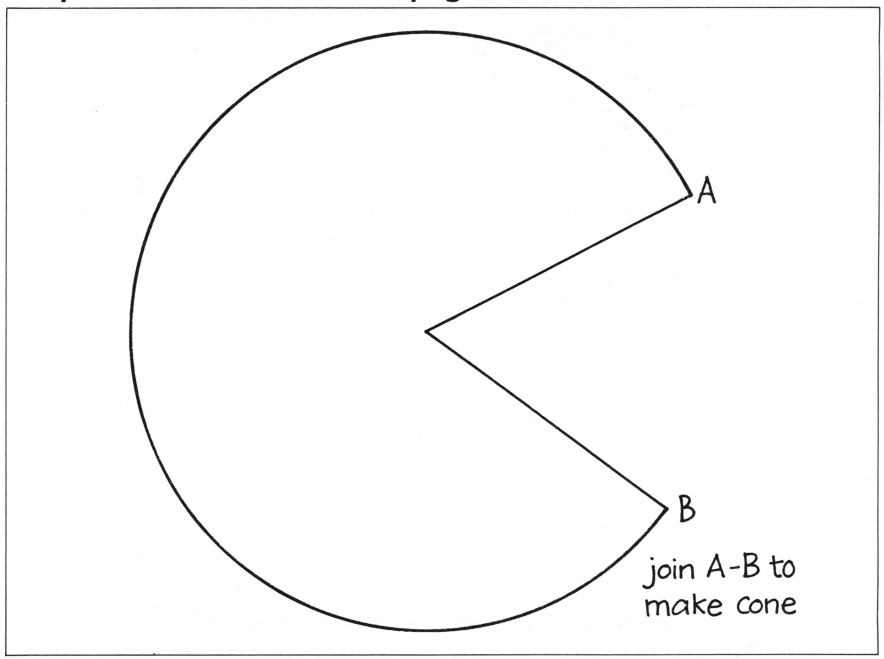

A

B

join A-B to
make cone

Template for Swan, see page 55

Template for Bird in a hoop, see page 67

Chart for feeding birds, see page 82

	Bird	Bacon	Fruit	Seeds	Nuts	Bread	Cheese

Chart for Looking at flowers, see page 90

Wild flowers							
Primrose	Bluebell	Cowslip	Wood anemone				

Chart for Flower spotting, see page 90

Garden flowers					
Daffodil	Snowdrop	Crocus	Tulip		

Flower chart, see page 91

Paschal lamb

Easter symbols

Chi-Rho

Latin cross

Greek cross

Celtic cross

A poem for Easter

Easter

Easter is a joyous time
Spring is in the air
Birds are building nests of twigs
New life is everywhere
There's crocuses and daffodils
And snowdrops by the score
There's Easter chicks
And bunnies too
And chocolate eggs galore

Easter is a special time
For wearing something new
For going out and having fun
There seems so much to do
Easter bonnets and parades
Playing sports and games
Eating special Easter food
With strange exciting names

And every year at Easter time,
People stop and pray
Remembering the risen Christ
On happy Easter Day

J Fitzsimmons

An Easter story

Blackie's Easter surprise

Jenny Flint was seven years old. She lived on a farm in New South Wales, Australia. She was a bright cheerful little girl, always smiling and happy, but she was happier than usual because Easter was just a week away and her mum and dad had promised to take her to the Royal Easter Show in Sydney. Sydney is one of the big cities of Australia and every year at Easter time, a big agricultural show is held there. In Australia the seasons are different, so Easter does not fall in spring, but at the end of summer.

Jenny knew that there would be lots of things to see. Her father was going especially to look at the livestock and new machinery, but Jenny had a special reason for going. She was going to take part in the Easter bonnet parade. She had already spent a great deal of time making her bonnet. She had used one of her mother's sun hats. It had a very wide brim and Jenny had made lots of paper flowers and stuck them all over the hat. Around the crown of the hat she had tied a beautiful pink satin sash in a great big bow, and the effect when she had finished was really very good indeed. When she had shown her mother the hat, she was really pleased that her mother said how beautiful it was. They looked for a box large enough to hold the hat so that it would be protected until they reached the showground.

After some searching they managed to find a suitable box and Jenny carefully put the hat inside. There was only a few days to go before the show and Jenny was getting impatient. The week seemed to last forever and no matter what she did to occupy herself, nothing seemed to make it go any faster.

Jenny had a cat called Blackie, and Blackie loved Jenny more than anything; he followed her everywhere and she loved to play with him but because she was anxious for Easter to arrive even Blackie didn't help.

At last Easter did arrive, and Jenny got up very early to hunt for her Easter eggs. Blackie helped and he was very good because he could sniff out chocolate very easily.

They had a lovely day. Jenny's friend Linda, who lived on the neighbouring farm, came over with her parents for a barbecue. In the late afternoon they sat on the steps at the back of the farm house munching chicken and sausages. Jenny told Linda about the Easter show and about the Easter bonnet parade. Linda wanted to see Jenny's hat. 'I'll show you', said Jenny, 'come on.'

They went to the box and Jenny carefully took the hat out and put it on.

'Oh it's lovely!' shouted Linda, 'you're sure to win.' 'That would be great', said Jenny, 'but we'll have to wait and see.'

Blackie miaowed as if to say, 'Of course it will win.' Jenny put the hat back in its box.

Because they had to make an early start next day, the barbecue didn't go on too late, and it was early evening when Jenny was tucked up in bed. At first she was too excited to sleep, but gradually her eyelids became heavy and she fell sound asleep. Before she knew it she was awakened by the sun streaming in at her bedroom window.

Normally Jenny took quite a long time to get up out of bed, but today it was quite different and she was up, washed and dressed quicker than a flash. She decided to wear her best dress for the Easter bonnet parade.

Jenny's father had loaded their big estate car while she was having breakfast and it wasn't long before they were ready to leave.

'Where's Blackie?' said Jenny. 'I must say goodbye to him.'

'I expect he's sulking somewhere because we're leaving him behind', said Mrs Flint.

'We'll only be away until tonight', said Mr Flint. 'You'll see him then. Now we really must be leaving, otherwise there will be no point in going at all.'

Reluctantly Jenny agreed and they set off. Soon they were heading down the highway towards Sydney and it wasn't long before they reached the showground and found a place to park. They decided to have a drink before going in. Mr Flint went round to the back of the car and lifted the rear door. As he was reaching for the flasks which Jenny's mother had prepared he did not

notice a black shape creep quietly from the car and disappear into the crowd.

After their drink, Jenny and her parents went into the showground and the first thing they did was to fill in the entry form for the Easter bonnet parade. This was due to take place at 1 o' clock. It was just after 9 o' clock so they had plenty of time to look around before getting ready for it.

They began their tour of the exhibits; there was so much to see. They looked at the latest farm machinery, and then saw some of the livestock being judged. Jenny's mother was interested in the exhibitions of fruit and vegetables, while Jenny thought the funfair was the most exciting thing of all. There were so many things to see that the time flew by and before anyone knew it, it was time for Jenny to get ready for the parade.

They went back to the car and Mr Flint reached into the back for the box containing Jenny's hat. She carefully pulled it out, but oh!! what a shock. The paper flowers that she had taken so much time and care over were all squashed and some were torn. The beautiful pink ribbon was missing, the hat was a mess! 'Oh, mother, who could have done such a thing?' said Jenny. She was so disappointed that she began to cry. 'Now, now!' said her mother. 'Let's see if we can try and repair it.' But no matter what they did, the hat was ruined.

Jenny was very sad, she had been so looking forward to the parade and now there was no hope of her entering the competition at all.

It was a mystery; what a dreadful thing to happen. Not even the biggest ice-cream could make Jenny feel better. Although she put on a very brave face and said that she

Blackie had wandered around the showground with the big pink ribbon fastened around his neck and was having a marvellous time sniffing and looking at all the interesting things around him.

At last he came to a large tent; inside he could hear the sounds of other cats. He walked in and looked around. There were cats of all kinds being brushed and patted and stroked by their owners. Some were sitting on large velvet cushions looking very grand.

There was a special compartment for each cat and its owner was standing by its side waiting patiently. A group of men and women were going from cat to cat and looking very carefully, then talking with its owner. Blackie was just about to walk away when two strong arms picked him up and put him in one of the compartments. He then heard a voice say, 'I thought number 276 had withdrawn. This must be it. I wonder where the owner is, the judges will be here soon.' The men walked on and it was at that moment that Jenny and her parents came into the tent. They were walking along the row of cats when Jenny suddenly stopped.

'Blackie!!' she gasped. 'It's Blackie, and he's wearing my ribbon.'

Blackie recognised Jenny at once and gave his loudest miaow.

'But how did he get here?' asked Mrs Flint. 'I think I know', said Mr Flint.

Just then one of the officials came up and said, 'The judges are coming, are you ready sir?'

Before they could say another word, the team of judges were looking closely at Blackie.

didn't mind at all, deep inside she was very sad, and the show seemed to have lost some of its magic.

Meanwhile, what about the black shape that had crawled from the back of the car when Jenny's father had opened it? You've probably guessed, it was Blackie. He had crawled into the box where Jenny's hat had been. He had thought it a lovely place to sleep especially when he had settled himself down and removed one or two lumps and bumps. He had been fast asleep when Jenny's father had loaded up the car that morning, and that was why he couldn't be found anywhere when Jenny had wanted to say goodbye.

'Lovely', said one.

'Marvellous', said another.

'This is the one!' said the third.

Jenny could not believe it when the last judge said, 'Is this your cat?' She nodded.

'Well its a credit to you my dear', said the first judge, 'well done.'

Mr Flint sorted out with the officials Blackie's entry into the cat show and everyone was overjoyed when an announcement came over the loudspeakers:

'First prize in the children's pet category goes to Blackie, Number 276, owned by Miss Jennifer Flint.'

'Hoorah!!' shouted Jenny, 'good old Blackie.'

'Now we know who spoiled the hat, it must have been a pretty good sleeping place for old Blackie', said Jenny's father.

Jenny hugged Blackie; this more than made up for the disappointment of the hat.

Blackie just purred; he didn't know what all the fuss was about, he was just glad to be with Jenny once more.

They received a beautiful golden rosette for Blackie, and also a certificate saying 'Best Pet in Show'.

There was still lots to do and see, and as soon as they had settled Blackie down in the car they went to see as many of the other exhibits as they could.

As they drove home that night, Jenny was thinking of all the exciting things that had taken place. A day which began so badly, but ended so very happily.

You can be sure that Blackie had a huge dish of cream and a plate of fish when they got home, and Jenny could only think what a lucky black cat he was, in more ways than one.

J Fitzsimmons

Resources

Books for teachers

The Easter Book compiled by Felicity Trotman (Hippo) – a fun activity book for children.

Easter the World over Priscilla Sawyer Lord and Daniel J Foley (Chilton Book Co) – a useful guide to Easter around the world.

Bright Ideas Seasonal Activities compiled by Janet Eyre (Scholastic Publications Ltd) – includes a section of ideas for spring and Easter.

The Easter Book Jenny Vaughan (Macdonald Educational) – looks at Easter and spring festivals in different countries, recipes, things to do and make, stories and poems.

Things to Make and Do for Easter Mariana Olivia Cole (Franklin Watts) – a useful source book for ideas.

Festivals 3 Jean Gilbert (OUP music) – includes a section on Easter.

Pancakes and Painted Eggs Jean Chapman (Hodder & Stoughton) – a compendium of activities for children.

Festive Occasions in the Primary School Redvers Brandling (Ward Lock Educational) – includes a section on Easter.

Books for children

The Easter Story by Jenny Robertson (Ladybird Bible Book)
The Spring Activity Book Susan Vesey (Lion Publishing)
Hare and the Easter Eggs Alison Uttley (Collins)
Little Grey Rabbit's Pancake Day Alison Uttley (Collins)

Music
Easter Parade Irving Berlin
The Seasons: Spring Vivaldi
Messiah Handel
Spring Song Mendelssohn

Suppliers
Beads and sequins can be bought by mail order or in person from:
Ells and Farrier,
5 Princes Street,
London W1

Hinges can be obtained from:
Cotswold Crafts
5 Whitehall,
Stroud,
Gloucestershire

A range of Easter festival rubber stamps can be obtained from:
Philip and Tracey,
North Way,
Andover,
Hampshire
S19 5BN

A filmstrip with an accompanying audio-cassette and teacher's book can be ordered from:
Mary Glasgow Publications,
Brookhampton Lane,
Kineton,
Warwickshire
CV35 OJB

Pictorial charts and information leaflets on Easter can be obtained from:
Pictorial Charts Educational Trust,
27 Kirchen Road,
London W13

Further information may be obtained from the chairperson and founder of the Egg Crafter's Guild:
Joan Cutts,
7 Hylton Terrace,
North Shields,
Tyne & Wear.

Acknowledgements

The editors and publishers extend grateful thanks for the reuse of material first published in *Art and Craft* to: Susan Mosey for 'Batik'; Andrew Listan for 'Striped eggs', 'Yarn eggs', 'Eggshell paperweights', 'An Easter rabbit' and 'Egg balloons'; Ann Hooke for 'Cutting eggs'; Margaret Greenwood for 'A Red Indian', 'Swan' and 'Bird in a hoop'; Warren Farnworth, Frank Peacock and Susan Mosey for 'Candle moulds'; Gloria Wittke for 'Egg and cress characters' and 'Easter tree'; Warren Farnworth for 'Eggshell caterpillar'; Joy Field for 'Chick box'; Patricia de Menezes for 'Posy basket', 'Cone basket' and 'Chicken in a basket'; G Roland Smith for 'Basket'; Alan and Gill Bridgewater for 'Easter egg wrapping paper'; Jan Messent for 'Mexican God's eye'; Anthony Hearne for 'Pecking birds'; Eileen Geipel for 'Easter bunny'; Sue Lawrence for 'Papier mâché hats'; Bob Neill for 'Bonnet', 'Cone hat' and 'Headbands'; Roberta Leslie for 'Easter doily bonnet'.

Also the National Christian Education Council for 'Table centre' from Ann Farncombe's *Easter Book*.

Every effort has been made to trace and acknowledge contributors. If any right has been omitted, the publishers offer their apologies and will rectify this in subsequent editions following notification.

Other books in the series

Previous titles in this series available are:

Bright Ideas Assemblies
0 590 70693 4   £5.45

Bright Ideas Classroom Management
0 590 70602 0   £5.45

Bright Ideas Christmas Activities
0 590 70803 1   £5.45

Bright Ideas Christmas Art & Craft
0 590 70832 5   £5.45

More Bright Ideas Christmas Art & Craft
0 590 70601 2   £5.45

Bright Ideas Crafty Moneymakers
0 590 70689 6   £5.45

Bright Ideas Games for PE
0 590 70690 X   £5.45

Bright Ideas History
0 590 70804 X   £5.45

Bright Ideas Language Development
0 590 70834 1   £5.45

Bright Ideas Lifesavers
0 590 70694 2   £5.45

Bright Ideas Maths Activities
0 590 70534 2   £5.45

Bright Ideas Maths Games
0 590 70874 0   £5.45

Bright Ideas Reading Activities
0 590 70535 0   £5.45

Bright Ideas Seasonal Activities
0 590 70831 7   £5.45

Bright Ideas Science
0 590 70833 3   £5.45

Bright Ideas Spelling
0 590 70802 3   £5.45

Bright Ideas Writing
0 590 70701 9   £5.45

Write to Scholastic Publications Ltd,
Westfield Road, Southam, Leamington Spa,
Warwickshire CV33 0JH. Enclose your
remittance. Make cheques payable to
Scholastic Publications Ltd.